CHINESE
in 10 minutes a day®

By **Kristine Kershul**, M.A., University of California, Santa Barbara

Third Edition
Special Consultant: Fu Tan
Book Editor: Fran Feldman

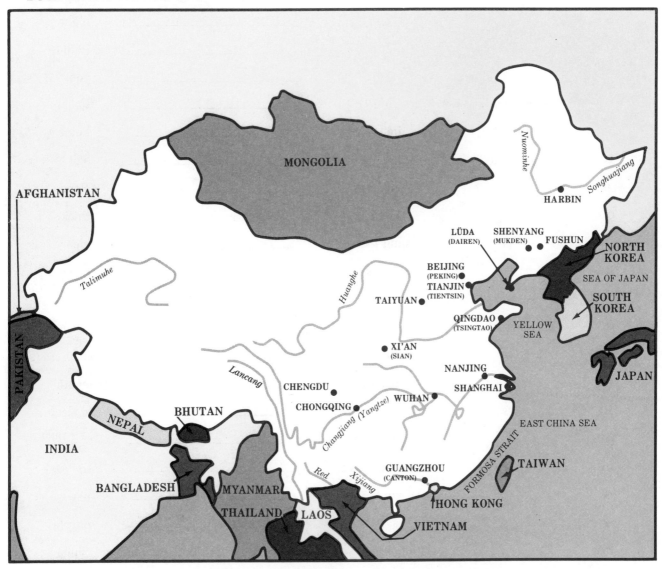

A Sunset Series

Sunset Publishing Corporation
Menlo Park, CA 94025

Second printing November 1994

(peen-yeen)
Pīnyīn
tool

Pīnyīn is a tool to help people read Chinese easily. To learn the Chinese sound of these letters, write each example in the space provided.

Pīnyīn	English sound	Example	*(Write it here)*	Meaning
a	ah	**chāzi** *(chah-zr)*	chāzi	fork
ai	i/y	**Shànghǎi** *(shahng-hi)*		Shanghai
ao	ow	**hǎo** *(how)*		good
c	ts *(as in its)*	**cǎo** *(tsow)*		grass
e	uh	**hē** *(huh)*		to drink
e	eh *(after y,u,i)*	**yè** *(yeh)*		night
ei	a/ay	**Běijīng** *(bay-jeeng)*		Beijing
i	ee	**nǐ** *(nee)*		you
i	r *(after c,ch,r,s,sh,z,zh)*	**chī** *(chr)*		to eat
ia	ee-ah	**jīa** *(jee-ah)*		home
iu	ee-oh	**qíu** *(chee-oh)*		ball
o	wo	**pō** *(pwo)*		slope
ou	oh	**hòu** *(hoh)*	hòu	thick
q	ch	**qīng** *(cheeng)*		clear
u	oo	**shū** *(shoo)*		book
u *(after j,q,x,y)* **or ü**	yew	**yú** *(yew)*		fish
ua	wah	**shūazi** *(shwah-zr)*		brush
uai	wy	**kùaizi** *(kwy-zr)*		chopstick(s)
ue	yew-eh	**yùe** *(yew-eh)*		month
ui	way	**shùi** *(shway)*		to sleep
un	oon yewn	**tūn** *(toon)* **yún** *(yewn)*		to swallow cloud
uo	wo	**shūo** *(shwo)*		to speak
x	ss	**xīn** *(sseen)*		new
z	z	**zǐ** *(zr)*		purple
zh	j	**Zhōnggúo** *(jung-gwo)*		China

Chinese is a tonal language with four basic tones.
1. The voice produces a flat, high pitch (—).
2. The voice rises from middle pitch to high pitch (/).
3. The voice drops from mid-low pitch to low pitch and then rises to mid-high pitch (˅).
4. The voice falls from high pitch to low pitch (\).

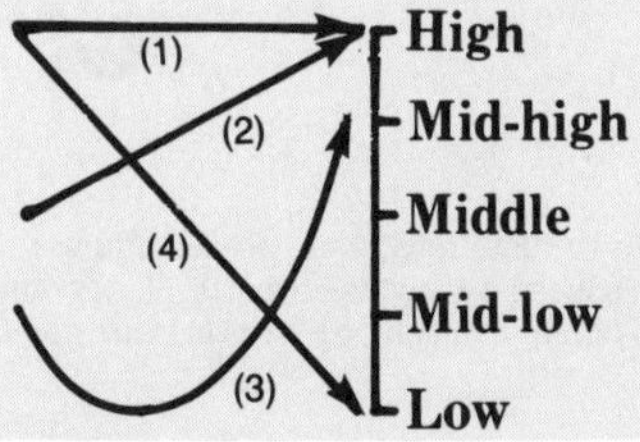

Nine Key Question Words

When you arrive in **Běijīng,** (bay-jeeng) / Peking the very first thing you will need to do is to ask questions — "Where is the train station?" "Where can I exchange money?" "Where (nahr) **(nǎr)** is the lavatory?" "**Nǎr** (nahr) / where is a restaurant?" "**Nǎr** do I catch a taxi?" "**Nǎr** is a good hotel?" "**Nǎr** is my luggage?" — and the list will go on and on for the entire length of your visit. In Chinese, there are NINE KEY QUESTION WORDS to learn. With these nine **cí,** (tsr) / words you can ask questions correctly. They will help you find out what you are ordering in a restaurant before you order it and not after the surprise (or shock!) arrives. These **cí** (tsr) / words are extremely important, so learn them now.

Take a few minutes to study and practice saying the nine question **cí** (tsr) listed below. Then cover the **cí** (tsr) with your hand and fill in each of the blanks with the matching Chinese **cí.** (tsr) / word

1.	**NǍR** (nahr)	= WHERE	_____
2.	**SHÉNME** (shun-muh)	= WHAT	_____
3.	**SHÉI** (shay)	= WHO	*shéi, shéi, shéi*
4.	**WÈISHÉNME** (way-shun-muh)	= WHY	_____
5.	**SHÉNME SHÍHÒU** (shun-muh) (shr-hoh)	= WHEN	_____
6.	**ZĚNME** (zuhn-muh)	= HOW	_____
7.	**DUŌSHǍO** (dwo-show)	= HOW MUCH HOW MANY	_____
8.	**JǏ** (jee)	= HOW MANY	_____
9.	**NÈI (NǍ)** (nay) (nah)	= WHICH	_____

Now test yourself to see if you really can keep these *(tsr)* **cí** straight in your mind. Draw lines

between the *(jung-wuhn)* **Zhōngwén** *(tsr)* **cí** and their English equivalents below.
Chinese   words

(nahr)
nǎr   who

(nay) (nah)
něi (nǎ)   how many

(shun-muh)
shénme   where

(shay)
shéi   why

(way-shun-muh)
wèishénme   how

(shun-muh) (shr-hoh)
shénme shíhòu   what

(zuhn-muh)
zěnme   which

(dwo-show)
dūoshǎo   how much

(jee)
jǐ   when

Examine the following questions containing these **cí.** Practice the sentences out loud and

then quiz yourself by filling in the blanks below with the correct question **cí.**

(dee-ahn-hwah) (zi) (nahr)
Dìanhùa zài nǎr? 电话
Where is the telephone?

(nah) (shr) (shay)
Nà shì shéi?
Who is that?

(hwo-chuh) (shun-muh) (shr-hoh)
Hǔochē shénme shíhòu
(li)
lái? 火车
What time does the train come?

(juh) (guh) (dwo-show) (chee-ahn)
Zhè ge dūoshǎo qían?
How much money is this?

(zuhn-muh) (luh)
Zěnme le?
What's wrong?

(sah-lah)(zuhn-muh)(yahng)
Sālā zěnme yàng?
How is the salad?

(nah) (guh)(nahn-ruhn)(shun-muh) (shr-hoh) (li)
Nà gē nánrén shénme shíhòu lái?
What time does that man come?

(way-shun-muh) (hwo-chuh) (boo) (li)
Wèishénme hǔochē bù lái?
Why does the train not come?

1. *(dee-ahn-hwah) (zi)* **Dìanhùa zài** _____ ?

2. *(nah) (shr)* **Nà shì** _____ ?

3. *(hwo-chuh)* **Hǔochē** *shénme shíhòu* *(li)* **lái?**

4. *(juh) (guh)* **Zhè ge** _____ *(chee-ahn)* **qían?**

5. _____ *(luh)* **le?**

6. *(sah-lah)* **Sālā** _____ *(yahng)* **yàng?**

7. *(nah) (guh) (nahn-ruhn)* **Nà ge nánrén** _____ *(li)* **lái?**

8. _____ *(hwo-chuh) (boo) (li)* **hǔochē bù lái?**

(nahr)
Nǎr will be your most used question **cí,** so let's concentrate on it. Say each of the

(jung-wuhn)
following **Zhōngwén** sentences aloud. Then write out each sentence without looking at the
Chinese

example. If you don't succeed on the first try, don't give up. Just practice each sentence

until you are able to do it easily.

Don't forget that you pronounce "**ai**" like "eye" and "**ia**" like "ee-ah." Also, use your

(peen-yeen)
4 pinyin when new **cí** are introduced.

(nahɹ) (yoh) (tsuh-swo)
Nǎr yǒu cèsuǒ?
where is   lavatory 厕所

MEN   WOMEN

(nahr) (yoh) (choo-zoo-chuh)
Nǎr yǒu chūzūchē?
where is   taxi 出租车

(yoh) (goong-goong-chee-chuh)
Nǎr yǒu gōnggòngqìchē?
(public) bus 公共汽车

(fahn-gwahnr)
Nǎr yǒu fànguǎnr?
restaurant 饭馆

(yeen-hahng)
Nǎr yǒu yínháng?
bank 银行

(lɘw-gwahn)
Nǎr yǒu lǚguǎn?
hotel 旅馆

Questions and answers are similar in Chinese. Here is an example.

(nahr) (yoh) (tsuh-swo)
Nǎr yǒu cèsuǒ? (question)
where   lavatory

(juhr)
Zhèr yǒu cèsuǒ. (answer)
here

(shun-muh)
Shénme is also a very useful question **cí.** From **shénme,** you can make other question
what

word combinations. Let's learn them now.

shénme shíhòu *(shr-hoh)* = when   **shénme dìfāng** *(dee-fahng)* = what   **shénme rén** *(ruhn)* = what person
                                                                place (where)   (who)

Below are more **cí** for you to learn as you work your way through this **shū.** *(shoo)*
book

Practice using the **Zhōngwén** tones (review page 2) with these new **cí.**

- ☑ **chāzi** *(chah-zr)* . . . . fork   *chāzi*
- ☑ **dāozi** *(dow-zr)* . . . . knife   筷子
- ☑ **kùaizi** *(kwy-zr)* . . . . chopsticks   *kuaizi*
- ☑ **pánzi** *(pahn-zr)* . . . . plate

Additional fun **cí** will appear at the bottom of the following pages in a yellow color band.

Be sure to say each **cí** aloud and then write out the **Zhōngwén cí** in the blank to the right. *(jung-wuhn)*
Chinese

5

Step 2

(juh)   *(nah)*
Zhè and **Nà**

The **Zhōngguó hùa** *(hwah)* / language does not have **cí** for "the" and "a." Instead, **zhè** *(juh)* and **nà** *(nah)* are used.

zhè *(juh)* = this, these   **nà** *(nah)* = that, those

In the **Zhōngguó hùa**, **zhè** *(juh)* and **nà** *(nah)* reflect the article's distance from the speaker.

zhè shū *(juh)(shoo)* / this book   vs.   **nà shū** / that book

zhè jī *(jee)* / chicken   vs.   **nà jī**

zhè yú *(yew)* / fish   vs.   **nà yú**

zhè dìanhùa *(dee-ahn-hwah)* / telephone   vs.   **nà dìanhùa**

In addition to **zhè** *(juh)* and **nà,** *(nah)* Chinese has "counting words" for everything. These are generally numbers like "one" room or quantities like "piece" of paper. **Běn** *(buhn)* is an example of a Chinese counting **cí**. **Běn,** *(buhn)* meaning "bound together," is used with words like "book" and "magazine."

yì běn shū *(yee)(buhn)(shoo)* / one bound book

yì běn zázhì *(yee)(buhn)(zah-jr)* / one bound magazine

Often, Chinese counting words cannot be translated into English. These counting words will be marked **(C)**.

Step 3

Dōngxi *(dwong-ssee)* / things

Before you proceed with this step, situate yourself comfortably in your living room. Now look around you. Can you name the things that you see in this **wūzi** *(woo-zr)* / room in Chinese? You can probably guess **shāfā** *(shah-fah)* means sofa, but let's learn the rest of them. After practicing these **cí** out loud, write them in the blanks below and on the next page.

hùar *(hwar)* = (the) picture   *hùar*

tīanhūabǎn *(tee-ahn-hwah-bahn)* = (the) ceiling _____

☐ **chē** *(chuh)* . . . . vehicle
☐ **chēfū** *(chuh-foo)* . . . . driver
☐ **chēlún** *(chun-loon)* . . . . wheel
☐ **chēfáng** *(chuh-fahng)* . . . . garage
☐ **chēzhàn** *(chuh-jahn)* . . . . bus stop

车 *che*

6

(chee-ahng-jee-ow)
qiángjiǎo = (the) corner _____

(chwahng-hoo)
chuānghù = (the) window _____

(dung)
dēng = (the) light _____

(ti-dung)
táidēng = (the) lamp _____

(shah-fah)
shāfā = (the) sofa _____

(yee-zr)
yǐzi = (the) chair _____

(dee-tahn)
dìtǎn = (the) carpet _____

(jwo-zr)
zhuōzi = (the) table _____

(muhn)
mén = (the) door _____

(jung)
zhōng = (the) clock _____

(chwahng-lee-ahn)
chuānglián = (the) curtain *chuānglián* _____

(chee-ahng)
qiáng = (the) wall _____

Remember that the **Zhōngguó** *(hwah)* **huà** has no "the." Use *(juh)* **zhè** or *(nah)* **nà** before the object to indicate
language   this   that

something in particular or use a number. Even easier, don't use anything at all. Now open

your *(shoo)* **shū** to the first page with the stick-on labels. Peel off the first 14 labels and
book

proceed around the room, labeling these items in your *(jee-ah)* **jiā.** This will help to increase your
home

Chinese vocabulary easily. Do not forget to say the **cí** as you attach each label.

Now ask yourself, "**Shāfā** *(shah-fah)* **zài** *(zi)* **nǎr**?" *(nahr)* and point to it while you answer, "**Shāfā** *(shah-fah)* **zài** *(zi)* **zhèr**." *(juhr)*
sofa   is   where   sofa   is

Continue on down the list until you feel comfortable with these **xīn cí.** *(sseen)* Say, "**Shū**
new   book

(zi) **zài** **nǎr**?" *(juhr)* Then reply, "**Shū zài** **zhèr**," and so on. When you can identify all the **dōngxi** *(dwong-ssee)*
things

on the list, you will be ready to move on.

Now, starting on the next page, let's learn some basic parts of the house.

☐ **diànchē** *(dee-ahn-chuh)*	trolley		_____
☐ **huǒchē** *(hwo-chuh)*	train		_____
☐ **qìchē** *(chee-chuh)*	car	车	_____
☐ **sānlúnchē** *(sahn-loon-chuh)*	pedicab	*che*	_____
☐ **zìxíngchē** *(zr-sseeng-chuh)*	bicycle		_____

7

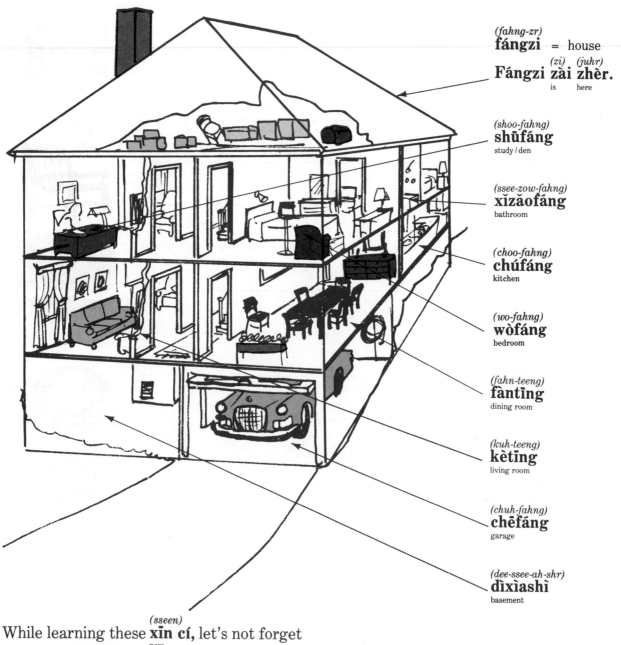

(fahng-zr)
fángzi = house

(zi) *(juhr)*
Fángzi zài zhèr.
is   here

(shoo-fahng)
shūfáng
study / den

(ssee-zow-fahng)
xǐzǎofáng
bathroom

(choo-fahng)
chúfáng
kitchen

(wo-fahng)
wòfáng
bedroom

(fahn-teeng)
fàntīng
dining room

(kuh-teeng)
kètīng
living room

(chuh-fahng)
chēfáng
garage

(dee-ssee-ah-shr)
dìxiàshì
basement

(sseen)
While learning these **xīn cí,** let's not forget
new

(chee-chuh)
qìchē
car

(zr-sseeng-chuh)
zìxíngchē
bicycle

(goh)
gǒu
dog

☐ **bǐ** *(bee)*	to write	
☐ **bǐjì** *(bee-jee)*	handwriting	笔
☐ **bǐjiān** *(bee-jee-ahn)*	pen nib	*bi*
☐ **bǐjìběn** *(bee-jee-buhn)*	notebook	
☐ **bǐzhě** *(bee-juh)*	writer, author	

(mow)
māo
cat

(hwah-yew-ahn)
hūayúan
garden

(sseen)
xìn
letters

_____   _____   *xìn*

(yoh-twong)
yóutǒng
mailbox

(hwar)
hūar (hùar means picture)
flowers

(muhn-leeng)
ménlíng
doorbell

_____   _____   _____

Peel off the next set of labels and wander through your *(fahng-zr)* **fángzi** learning these *(sseen)* **xìn** *(tsr)* **cí.**

house   new   words

Granted, it will be somewhat difficult to label your *(goh)* **gǒu,** *(mow)* **māo** or *(hwar)* **hūar,** but use your imagination.

Again, practice by asking yourself, "**Hūayúan** *(hwah-yew-ahn)(zi)* **zài** *(nahr)* **nǎr?**" or "**Nǎr** *(yoh)* **yǒu** **hūayúan?**"

is where   where is

and reply, "**Hūayúan zài** *(juhr)* **zhèr.**"

here

(nahr) (yoh)
Nǎr yǒu
where is

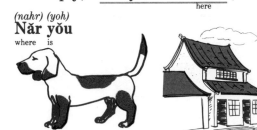   

☐ **fěnbǐ** *(fuhn-bee)* .... chalk
☐ **gāngbǐ** *(gahng-bee)* .... pen
☐ **máobǐ** *(mow-bee)* .... writing brush
☐ **qīanbǐ** *(chee-ahn-bee)* .... pencil
☐ **yúanzhūbǐ** *(yew-ahn-joo-bee)* .... ballpoint pen

笔
bi

_____

_____

Step 4

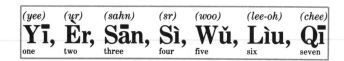

(yee)	(ur)	(sahn)	(sr)	(woo)	(lee-oh)	(chee)
Yī,	**Ěr,**	**Sān,**	**Sì,**	**Wǔ,**	**Lìu,**	**Qī**
one	two	three	four	five	six	seven

(yee) *(yee)* *(yee)* *(ur)* *(ur)* *(yee)* *(sahn)*
yī, yī, yī ěr, ěr yī, yī ěr sān, sān ěr yī,
one   two   three

(sr)(woo) (lee-oh) (chee)
yi ěr sān sì wǔ lìu   qī.
four five six   seven

In **Zhōngguó,** *(jung-gwo)* / China, as in America, children choose sides for games by reciting a counting rhyme

like the one above. In other ways, however, **shùzì** *(shoo-zr)* / numbers are used differently in the **Zhōngguó**

hùa. *(hwah)* / language Unlike English, in the **Zhōngguó hùa,** days and months are indicated by **shùzì.** *(shoo-zr)* / number

For example, **yī yùe,** *(yee) (yew-eh)* / month meaning one or first month, means January in the **Zhōngguó hùa.**

When learning the following **shùzì,** *(shoo-zr)* notice the similarities (underlined) between numbers

like **ěr** *(ur)* (2) and **shíěr** *(shr-ur)* (12), and **qī** *(chee)* (7) and **shíqī** *(shr-chee)* (17). After practicing the **shùzì** out loud,

cover the **Zhōngwén cí** and write the **shùzì** 1 through 10 in the blanks.

0	*(leeng)* **líng**			**0**	*líng*
1	*(yee)* **yī**	**11**	*(shr-yee)* **shíyī**	**1**	_____
2	*(ur)* **ěr**	**12**	*(shr-ur)* **shíèr**	**2**	_____
3	*(sahn)* **sān**	**13**	*(shr-sahn)* **shísān**	**3**	_____
4	*(sr)* **sì**	**14**	*(shr-sr)* **shísì**	**4**	_____
5	*(woo)* **wǔ**	**15**	*(shr-woo)* **shíwǔ**	**5**	_____
6	*(lee-oh)* **lìu**	**16**	*(shr-lee-oh)* **shílìu**	**6**	_____
7	*(chee)* **qī**	**17**	*(shr-chee)* **shíqī**	**7**	_____
8	*(bah)* **bā**	**18**	*(shr-bah)* **shíbā**	**8**	_____
9	*(jee-oh)* **jǐu**	**19**	*(shr-jee-oh)* **shíjǐu**	**9**	_____
10	*(shr)* **shí**	**20**	*(ur-shr)* **ěrshí**	**10**	_____

☐ **dìan** *(dee-ahn)* . . . . electricity
☐ **dìanbàng** *(dee-ahn-bahng)* . . . . flashlight
☐ **dìanbào** *(dee-ahn-bow)* . . . . telegram
☐ **dìanhùa** *(dee-ahn-hwah)* . . . . telephone
☐ **dìannǎo** *(dee-ahn-now)* . . . . computer

电
dian

_____
_____
_____
_____
_____

Use these **shùzì** on a daily basis. Remove the next **shí** *(shr)* / ten labels and use them to practice as often as you can. Now fill in the following blanks according to the **shùzì** given in the parentheses.

Note: This is a good time to start learning these two important phrases.

(wo) (ssee-ahng) (yow)		
wǒ xiǎng yào =	I would like	_____
(wo-muhn) (ssee-ahng) (yow)		
wǒmen xiǎng yào =	we would like	_____

(wo) (ssee-ahng) (yow)
Wǒ xiǎng yào _____ (15)   *(jahng)* **zhāng** sheets *(jr)* **zhǐ.** paper   *(dwo-show)* **Dǔoshǎo?** how much _____ (15)

Wǒ xiǎng yào _____ (10)   **zhāng** (C) **míngxìnpìan.** *(meeng-sseen-pee-ahn)* postcards 明信片   *(dwo-show)* **Dǔoshǎo?** _____ (10)

Wǒ xiǎng yào _____ (11)   **zhāng** (C) **yóupìao.** *(yoh-pee-ow)* stamps 邮票   **Dǔoshǎo?** _____ (11)

Wǒ xiǎng yào _bā_ (8)   **jiālún** *(jee-ah-loon)* gallons **qìyóu.** *(chee-yoh)* gasoline   **Dǔoshǎo?** _____ (8)

Wǒ xiǎng yào _____ (1)   **bēi** *(bay)* cup **júzishǔi.** *(jew-zr-shway)* orange juice   **Dǔoshǎo?** _____ (1)

(wo-muhn) (ssee-ahng) (yow)
Wǒmen xiǎng yào _____ (3)   **zhāng** *(jahng)* **xìpìao.** *(ssee-pee-ow)* theater tickets   **Dǔoshǎo?** _____ (3)

Wǒmen xiǎng yào _____ (4)   **bēi** *(bay)* cup **chá.** *(chah)* tea 茶   **Dǔoshǎo?** _____ (4)

Wǒmen xiǎng yào _____ (2)   **bēi** *(bay)* glass **píjǐu.** *(pee-jee-oh)* beer   **Dǔoshǎo?** _____ (2)

Wǒmen xiǎng yào _____ (12)   **ge** *(guh)* (C) **xīnxian** *(sseen-ssee-ahn)* fresh **jīdàn.** *(jee-dahn)* eggs   **Dǔoshǎo?** _____ (12)

Wǒmen xiǎng yào _____ (6)   **bàng** *(bahng)* pounds **ròu.** *(roh)* meat   **Dǔoshǎo?** _____ (6)

Wǒmen xiǎng yào _____ (5)   **bēi** *(bay)* **shǔi.** *(shway)* water   **Dǔoshǎo?** _____ (5)

Wǒmen xiǎng yào _____ (7)   **bēi** *(bay)* **jǐu.** *(jee-oh)* wine 酒   **Dǔoshǎo?** _qī_ (7)

Wǒmen xiǎng yào _____ (9)   **bàng** *(bahng)* **húangyóu.** *(hwahng-yoh)* (C) butter   **Dǔoshǎo?** _____ (9)

☐ **dìanshì** *(dee-ahn-shr)* .... television _____
☐ **dìantái** *(dee-ahn-ti)* .... radio station _____
☐ **dìantī** *(dee-ahn-tee)* .... elevator 电 _____
☐ **dìanyǐng** *(dee-ahn-yeeng)* .... movie *dian* _____
☐ **dìanzhōng** *(dee-ahn-jung)* .... electric clock _____

In **Zhōngwén, liǎng** (lee-ahng) also means two.

Now see if you can translate the following thoughts into **Zhōngwén** (jung-wuhn) Chinese. The answers are at the bottom of **zhè yè** (juh) (yeh) this page.

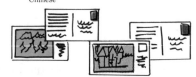

1.   I would like seven postcards.

_____

2.   I would like one beer.   _Wǒ xiǎng yào yì bēi píjiǔ._

3.   We would like two glasses of water.

_____

4.   We would like three theater tickets.

_____

Review the **shùzì** numbers 1 through 20 and answer the following questions aloud. Then write the answers in the blank spaces.

Zhèr yǒu dūoshǎo zhāng (juhr) (yoh) (dwo-show) (jahng) are
zhūozi? (jwo-zr) tables   _sān zhāng_

Zhèr yǒu dūoshǎo (juhr) here
ge táiděng? (guh)(ti-dung) (C)   _____

Zhèr yǒu dūoshǎo bǎ yǐzi? (bah)(yee-zr) (C)   _____

(juhr) (yoh) (dwo-show) (jung)
Zhèr yǒu duōshǎo zhǒng?
here   are   how many

_____

Zhèr yǒu jǐ ge chuānghù?
how many (C) _(jee)_ _(chwahng-hoo)_
how many (C)

_____

Zhèr yǒu jǐ ge rén?
(jee) _(ruhn)_
how many (C) people

liù

Zhèr yǒu jǐ ge nánrén?
(nahn-ruhn)
(C)   men

_____

Zhèr yǒu jǐ ge nǚrén?
(new-ruhn)
(C)   women

_____

(yahn-suh)
Yánsè
colors

Step 5

On the next page are the **míngzì** _(meeng-zr)_ of the **yánsè** _(yahn-suh)_ in **Zhōngwén.** In **Zhōngguó,** there
names   colors

are many different customs regarding **yánsè.** _(yahn-suh)_ For example, if you visit a **péngyǒu** _(pung-yoh)_ in the
colors   friend

hospital, you should take **huār** _(hwar)_ that are **hóng** _(hohng)_ or **huā.** _(hwah)_ Do not take **huār** that are **bái** _(bi)_ or
flowers   red   multi-colored   white

huáng—those colors are for mourning. Now let's learn the basic **yánsè.** Once you have
(hwahng)
yellow   colors

read through the list on the next **yè,** _(yeh)_ cover the **Zhōngwén cí** with your hand and practice
page

writing out the **Zhōngwén cí** next to the English **cí.**

☐ **méi** _(may)_ . . . . coal
☐ **méikuàng** _(may-kwahng)_ . . . . coal mine
☐ **méiqì** _(may-chee)_ . . . . gas
☐ **méiqìlú** _(may-chee-loo)_ . . . . gas stove
☐ **méiyóu** _(may-yoh)_ . . . . kerosene

煤
mei

_____
_____
_____
_____
_____

(bi)
bái = white _____ *(chwahn)* *(shr)(bi-duh)*
Chúan shì báide.
boat   is

(hay)
hēi = black _____ *(chee-yoh)* *(hay-duh)*
Qíu shì hēide.
ball

(hwahng)
húang = yellow _____ *(ssee-ahng-jee-ow)* *(hwahng-duh)*
Xiangjiao shì húangde.
banana

(hohng)
hóng = red ___ *hóng* ___ *(shoo)* *(hohng-duh)*
Shú shì hóngde.
book

(lahn)
lán = blue _____ *(chee-chuh)* *(lahn-duh)*
Qìchē shì lánde.
car

(hway)
hūi = gray _____ *(ssee-ahng)* *(hway-duh)*
Xìang shì hūide.
elephant

(kah-fay-suh)
kāfēisè = brown _____ *(yee-zr)* *(kah-fay-suh-duh)*
Yǐzi shì kāfēisède.
chair

(lew)
lǜ = green _____ *(tsow)* *(lew-duh)*
Cǎo shì lǜde.
grass

(fuhn)
fěn = pink _____ *(hwar)* *(fuhn-duh)*
Hūar shì fěnde.
flower

(hwah)
hūa = multi-colored _____ *(ti-dung)* *(hwah-duh)*
Táidēng shì hǔade.
lamp

Now peel off the next set of labels and proceed to label the *(yahn-suh)* **yánsè** in your *(fahng-zr)* **fángzi.** Now
colors   house

let's practice using *(juh) (ssee-eh)* **zhè xīe cí.**
these several

(chwahn) (zi) (nahr)
Bái chúan zài nǎr? ___ *Bái* ___ *(zi) (nahr)* **chúan zài nàr.**
boat   is   where   is   there

(jwo-zr)
Hūi zhūozi zài nǎr? _____ **zhūozi zài nàr.**
table

(yee-zr)
Kāfēisè yǐzi zài nǎr? _____ **yǐzi zài nàr.**
chair

(chee-oh)
Bái qíu zài nǎr? _____ **qíu zài nàr.**
ball

(ti-dung)
Hūa táidēng zài nǎr? _____ **táidēng zài nàr.**
lamp

(shoo)
Hóng shú zài nǎr? _____ **shú zài nàr.**
book

☐ **dìan** *(dee-ahn)* . . . . store, shop _____
☐ **dìanyúan** *(dee-ahn-yew-ahn)* . . . . clerk _____
☐ **dìanzhǔ** *(dee-ahn-joo)* . . . . storekeeper 店 _____
☐ **gǔdǒng dìan** *(goo-dwong) (dee-ahn)* . . . . antique shop *dian* _____
14 ☐ **hūa dìan** *(hwah) (dee-ahn)* . . . . florist shop _____

(muhn) (zi) (nahr)
Lǚ mén zài nǎr?   _____ *(zi) (nahr)* **mén zài nàr.**
door is where   is there

(fahng-zr)
Fěn fángzi zài nǎr?   _____ **fángzi zài nàr.**
house

(ssee-ahng-jee-ow)
Húang xiāngjīao zài nǎr?   _____ **xiāngjīao zài nàr.**
banana

Note: In **Zhōngguó hùa**, "**yǒu**" *(yoh)* means both "to have" and "there is/are."

(wo) (yoh)
wǒ yǒu = I have _____   *(wo-mun) (yoh)* **wǒmen yǒu** = we have _____

(ssee-ahng) (yow) *(yoh)*
Let's review **xiǎng yào** and learn **yǒu**. Be sure to repeat each sentence out loud.

(wo) (ssee-ahng)(yow) (bay) (pee-jee-oh)
Wǒ xiǎng yào yì bēi píjǐu.
I would like one glass beer
(wo-muhn)   *(jee-oh)*
Wǒmen xiǎng yào liǎng bēi jǐu.
we   would like   wine

(shway)
Wǒ xiǎng yào yì bēi shǔi.
water
(guh) (sah-lah)
Wǒmen xiǎng yào yí ge sālā.
(C) salad

(chee-chuh)
Wǒmen xiǎng yào yí lìang qìchē.
(C)

(oh-joh)
Wǒmen xiǎng yào zài Ōuzhōu yǒu yí
to be in Europe   have

lìang qìchē.
(C) car

(yoh)
Wǒ yǒu yì bēi píjǐu.
I have beer

Wǒmen yǒu liǎng bēi jǐu.
have   wine

(swo) (fahng-zr)
Wǒ yǒu yì sǔo fángzi.
(C) house
(may-gwo)
Wǒ zài Měigúo yǒu yì sǔo fángzi.
am in

(zr-sseeng-chuh)
Wǒ yǒu yí lìang zìxíngchē.
(C)   bicycle

(oh-joh)
Wǒmen zài Ōuzhōu yǒu yí
       Europe
lìang qìchē.
(C) car

Now fill in the following blanks with the correct **cí** of **yǒu** or **xiǎng yào**.
form

Wǒmen yǒu   *(chee-chuh)*
(we have)   **sān lìang qìchē.**
three

_____ *(jahng) (ssee-pee-ow)*
(we would like)   **liǎng zhāng xìpìao.**
two (C)

_____ *(hwar)*
(I have)   **yì zhāng hùar.**
one (C)

_____ *(meeng-sseen-pee-ahn)*
(I would like)   **qī zhāng míngxìnpìan.**
seven (C)

☐ **lǐfà dìan** *(lee-fah) (dee-ahn)* . . . . hairdresser's
☐ **ròu dìan** *(roh) (dee-ahn)* . . . . butcher shop
☐ **shū dìan** *(shoo) (dee-ahn)* . . . . bookstore
☐ **yào dìan** *(yow) (dee-ahn)* . . . . pharmacy
☐ **xíe dìan** *(ssee-eh) (dee-ahn)* . . . . shoe store

店
dian

_____
_____
_____
_____

15

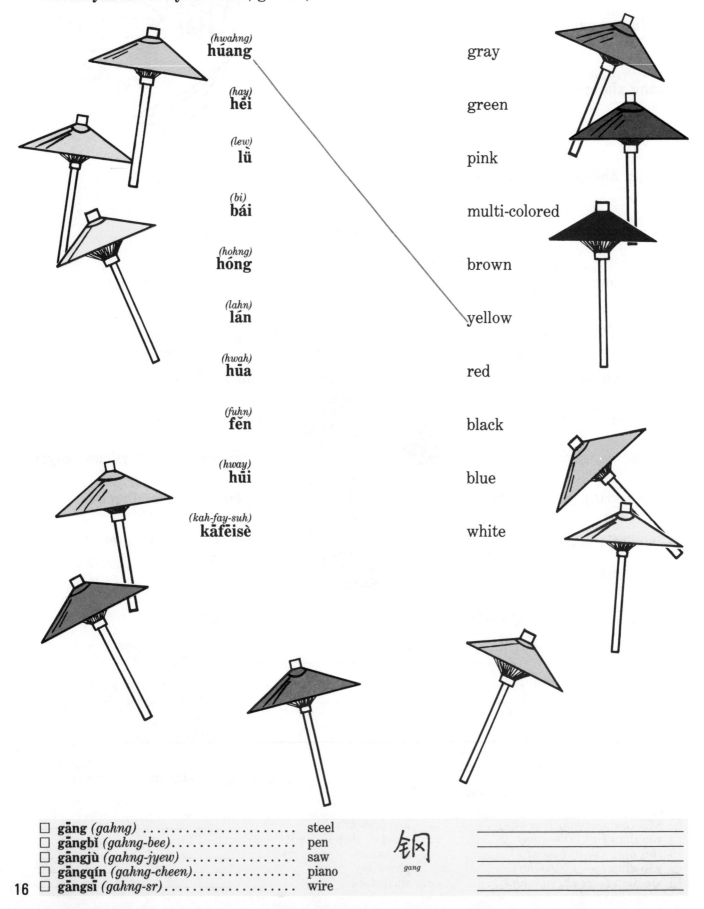

Zhèr yǒu yí ge quick review of the **yánsè.** Draw lines between the **Zhōngwén cí** and the
(juhr) *(yoh)*
here is (C) colors

correct **yánsè.** On your mark, get set, *GO!*

(hwahng) **húang**

(hay) **hēi**

(lew) **lü**

(bi) **bái**

(hohng) **hóng**

(lahn) **lán**

(hwah) **hūa**

(fuhn) **fěn**

(hway) **hūi**

(kah-fay-suh) **kāfēisè**

gray

green

pink

multi-colored

brown

yellow

red

black

blue

white

☐ **gāng** *(gahng)* . . . . steel
☐ **gāngbǐ** *(gahng-bee)* . . . . pen
☐ **gāngjù** *(gahng-jyew)* . . . . saw
☐ **gāngqín** *(gahng-cheen)* . . . . piano
☐ **gāngsī** *(gahng-sr)* . . . . wire

钢
gang

16

Before starting this step, go back and review Step 4. Make sure you can count to **èrshí** *(ur-shr)* twenty

without looking back at the **shū**. *(shoo)* book Let's learn the larger **shùzì** *(shoo-zr)* numbers now, so if something

costs more than 20 **yúan,** *(yew-ahn)* you will know exactly how much it costs. After practicing aloud

the **Zhōngwén** *(jung-wuhn)* Chinese **shùzì** *(shoo-zr)* numbers below, write these **shùzì** *(shoo-zr)* in the blanks provided. Again, notice the

similarities between numbers such as **wǔshí** *(woo-shr)* (50), **wǔ** *(woo)* (5) and **shíwǔ** *(shr-woo)* (15).

10	**shí** *(shr)*			
20	**èrshí** *(ur-shr)*	**èr** *(ur)*	=	2)
30	**sānshí** *(sahn-shr)*	**sān** *(sahn)*	=	3)
40	**sìshí** *(sr-shr)*	**sì** *(sr)*	=	4)
50	**wǔshí** *(woo-shr)*	**wǔ** *(woo)*	=	5)
60	**lìushí** *(lee-oh-shr)*	**lìu** *(lee-oh)*	=	6)
70	**qīshí** *(chee-shr)*	**qī** *(chee)*	=	7)
80	**bāshí** *(bah-shr)*	**bā** *(bah)*	=	8)
90	**jǐushí** *(jee-oh-shr)*	**jǐu** *(jee-oh)*	=	9)
100	**yībǎi** *(yee-bi)*			
1000	**yīqīan** *(yee-chee-ahn)*			

10 _____ *shí* _____

20 _____

30 _____

40 _____

50 _____

60 _____

70 _____

80 _____

90 _____

100 _____

1000 _____

Now take a logical guess. **Zěnme** *(zuhn-muh)* how would you write (and say) the following? The answers

zài *(zi)* are at the bottom of **zhèi** *(jay)* this **yè.** *(yeh)* page

400 _____

600 _____

2000 _____

5300 _____

The unit of currency in **Zhōngguó** *(jung-gwo)* is the **yúan** *(yew-ahn)*. Currency is called **zhǐbì** *(jr-bee)* and coins are called **yìngbì** *(yeeng-bee)*. Just as in **Měiguó** *(may-gwo)* where a dollar can be broken down into 100 pennies, the **yúan** *(yew-ahn)* can be divided into 100 **fēn** *(fuhn)*. The **yúan** *(yew-ahn)* can also be broken down into 10 **jǐao** *(jee-ow)*, or **máo** *(mow)*. **Jǐao** *(jee-ow)*, or **máo** *(mow)*, and **fēn** *(fuhn)* are also called **fǔbì** *(foo-bee)*. Let's learn the various kinds of **zhǐbì** *(jr-bee)* and **yìngbì** *(yeeng-bee)*. Because you will not be able to exchange American currency for **yúan**

until you are actually in China, study the pictures below to familiarize yourself with the

various **zhǐbì** *(jr-bee)* and **yìngbì** *(yeeng-bee)*. Also make sure to practice each **cí** *(tsr)* out loud.
currency   coins   word

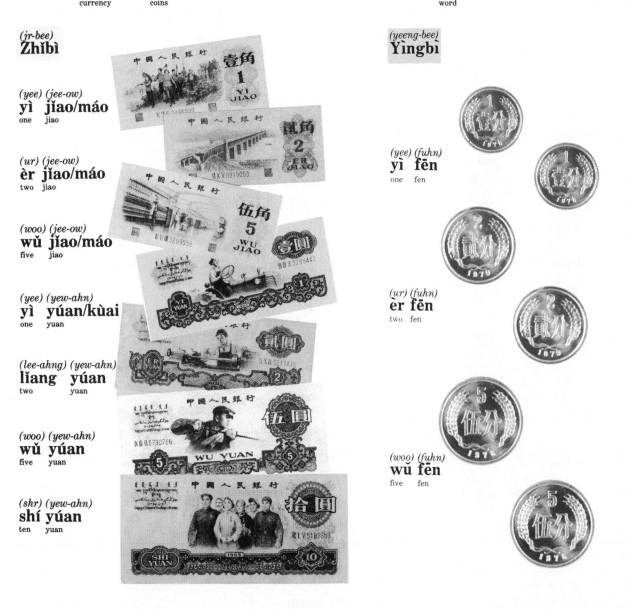

Zhǐbì *(jr-bee)*

yì jǐao/máo *(yee) (jee-ow)*
one   jiao

èr jǐao/máo *(ur) (jee-ow)*
two   jiao

wǔ jǐao/máo *(woo) (jee-ow)*
five   jiao

yì yúan/kùai *(yee) (yew-ahn)*
one   yuan

lǐang yúan *(lee-ahng) (yew-ahn)*
two   yuan

wǔ yúan *(woo) (yew-ahn)*
five   yuan

shí yúan *(shr) (yew-ahn)*
ten   yuan

Yìngbì *(yeeng-bee)*

yì fēn *(yee) (fuhn)*
one   fen

er fēn *(ur) (fuhn)*
two   fen

wǔ fēn *(woo) (fuhn)*
five   fen

☐ **nían** *(nee-ahn)* . . . . year
☐ **jīnnían** *(jeen-nee-ahn)* . . . . this year
☐ **míngnían** *(meeng-nee-ahn)* . . . . next year
☐ **qùnían** *(chyew-nee-ahn)* . . . . last year
☐ **sānnían** *(sahn-nee-ahn)* . . . . three years

年
nian

Review the **shùzì shí** *(shoo-zr) (shr)* through **yīqiān** *(yee-chee-ahn)* again. Now, in **Zhōngwén,** *(jung-wuhn)* **nǐ** *(nee)* **zěnme** *(zuhn-muh)* **shūo** *(shwo)*
numbers ten   one thousand   Chinese   you   how   say

"twenty-two" or "fifty-three"? You actually do a bit of arithmetic — 5 times 10 plus 3
wǔ   **shí**   **sān**

equals 53. See if you can say and write out the **shùzì** *(shoo-zr)* on **zhèi yè.** *(jay) (yeh)* The answers **zài** *(zi)*
wǔshísān   this   are at

the bottom of the **yè.** *(yeh)*
page

a. 25 = _ershíwǔ_____   e. 36 = _____
     (2 x 10) + 5   (3 x 10) + 6

b. 47 = _____   f. 93 = _____
     (4 x 10) + 7   (9 x 10) + 3

c. 84 = _____   g. 68 = _____
     (8 x 10) + 4   (6 x 10) + 8

d. 51 = _____   h. 72 = _____
     (5 x 10) + 1   (7 x 10) + 2

To ask how much something costs in the **Zhōngguó** *(jung-gwo)* **hùa,** *(hwah)* one asks, "**Dūoshǎo** *(dwo-show)* **qían?**" *(chee-ahn)*
Chinese   language   how much   money

Xìanzài *(ssee-ahn-zi)* answer the following questions based on the **shùzì** *(shoo-zr)* in parentheses.
now   numbers

1. **Nà shì dūoshǎo qían?** *(nah) (shr) (dwo-show) (chee-ahn)*   **Nà shì** *(nah)* _shí____ **yúan.** *(yew-ahn)*
   that (C) how much money   (10)

2. **Nà shì dūoshǎo qían?** *(nah) (shr) (dwo-show) (chee-ahn)*   **Nà shì** *(nah)* _____ **yúan.** *(yew-ahn)*
   that (C) how much money   (20)

3. **Nà běn shū dūoshǎo qían?** *(buhn) (shoo) (dwo-show) (chee-ahn)*   **Nà běn** _____ **yúan.**
   that (C) book   (17)

4. **Nà lìang qìchē dūoshǎo qían?** *(lee-ahng) (chee-chuh) (dwo-show)*   **Nà lìang** _____ **yúan.**
   (C) car   (2000)

5. **Nà zhāng zhàopìan dūoshǎo qían?** *(jahng) (jow-pee-ahn)*   **Nà zhāng** _____ **yúan.**
   (C) photo   (5)

6. **Nà jīan wūzi dūoshǎo qían?** *(jee-ahn) (woo-zr)*   **Nà jīan** _____ **yúan.**
   (C) room   (24)

7. **Nà zhāng hùar dūoshǎo qían?** *(jahng) (hwar)*   **Nà zhāng** _____ **yúan.**
   (C) picture   (923)

ANSWERS

7. jiǔbǎi èrshísān	2. èrshí	e. sānshíliù
6. èrshísì	1. shí	d. wǔshíyī
5. wǔ	h. qīshíèr	c. bāshísì
4. liǎngqian	g. liùshíbā	b. sìshíqī
3. shíqī	f. jiǔshísān	a. èrshíwǔ

Step 7

(jeen-tee-ahn) *(meeng-tee-ahn)* *(zwo-tee-ahn)*
Jīntiān, Míngtiān, Zúotiān
today   tomorrow   yesterday

(rr-lee)
Rìlì
calendar

(yee) (guh) (sseeng-chee) (yoh) (chee) (tee-ahn) **Yí ge xīngqi yǒu qī tiān.** one (C) week has seven days	

(sseeng-chee-yee) **xīngqiyi** 1	*(sseeng-chee-ur)* **xīngqièr** 2	*(sseeng-chee-sahn)* **xīngqisān** 3	*(sseeng-chee-sr)* **xīngqisì** 4	*(sseeng-chee-woo)* **xīngqiwǔ** 5	*(sseeng-chee-lee-oh)* **xīngqilìu** 6	*(sseeng-chee-tee-ahn)* **xīngqitian** 7

Notice that in *(jung-wuhn)* **Zhōngwén,** numbers are included in the names for weekdays. It is *(huhn)* **hěn** very

important to know these days. Be sure to say them aloud before filling in the blanks

below.

(sseeng-chee-yee)
xīngqiyi *xīngqīyī*
Monday

(sseeng-chee-ur)
xīngqièr
Tuesday

(sseeng-chee-sahn)
xīngqisān
Wednesday

(sseeng-chee-sr)
xīngqisì
Thursday

(sseeng-chee-woo)
xīngqiwǔ
Friday

(sseeng-chee-lee-oh)
xīngqilìu
Saturday

(sseeng-chee-tee-ahn)
xīngqitian
Sunday

If *(jeen-tee-ahn)* **jīntiān** today *(shr)* **shì** is *(sseeng-chee-sr)* **xīngqisì**, then *(meeng-tee-ahn)* **míngtiān** tomorrow **shì** is *(sseeng-chee-woo)* **xīngqiwǔ** Friday and *(zwo-tee-ahn)* **zúotiān** yesterday **shì** was *(sseeng-chee-sahn)* **xīngqisān**. Wednesday Now,

you supply the correct answers. If **jīntiān shì xīngqièr**, then **míngtiān shì** _____
today   Tuesday   tomorrow

and **zúotiān shì** _____. Or, if **jīntiān shì xīngqilìu**, then _____
today   Saturday

(sseeng-chee-tee-ahn)
shì xīngqitian and _____ *(sseeng-chee-woo)* **shì xīngqiwǔ.** Easy, wasn't it? **Jīntiān shì**
Sunday   Friday   today

_____.

(ssee-ahn-zi)
Xiānzǎi, peel off the next *(chee) (guh)* **qī ge** labels and put them on the *(rr-lee)* **rìlì** that you use every day.
now   seven (C)   calendar

(shr) (sseeng-chee-yee)
From now on, Monday **shì xīngqiyi!**
is

☐ **là** *(lah)*	. . . .	wax	_____
☐ **làbǐ** *(lah-bee)*	. . . .	crayon	_____
☐ **làtái** *(lah-ti)*	. . . .	candlestick	蜡 _____
☐ **làzhǐ** *(lah-jr)*	. . . .	waxed paper	*la* _____
☐ **làzhú** *(lah-joo)*	. . . .	candle	_____

20

There are **sì ge** *(sr)(guh)* parts to each **tiān.** *(tee-ahn)*
four (C) · day

morning = **shàngwǔ** *(shahng-woo)*	_____
afternoon = **xìawǔ** *(ssee-ah-woo)*	*xìawǔ* _____
evening = **wǎnshang** *(wahn-shahng)*	_____
night = **yèlǐ** *(yeh-lee)*	_____

Also, in **Zhōngwén,** *(jung-wuhn)* **báitiān** *(bi-tee-ahn)* means daytime. **Xìanzài,** *(ssee-ahn-zi)* fill in the following blanks
now
and then check your answers at the bottom of **zhèi yè.** *(jay)* *(yeh)*
this page

a. Sunday morning = _____

b. Friday evening = _____

c. Saturday evening = _____

d. Monday morning = _____

e. Wednesday morning = _____

f. Tuesday afternoon = _____

g. Thursday afternoon = _____

h. Thursday night = *xīngqīsì yèlǐ*

i. yesterday evening = _____

j. this afternoon = _____
(today)

k. this morning = _____

l. tomorrow afternoon = _____

m. tomorrow evening = _____

ANSWERS

a. xīngqītiān shàngwǔ	e. xīngqīsān shàngwǔ	i. zuótiān wǎnshàng
b. xīngqīwǔ wǎnshàng	f. xīngqīèr xìawǔ	j. jīntiān xìawǔ
c. xīngqīliù wǎnshàng	g. xīngqīsì xìawǔ	k. jīntiān shàngwǔ
d. xīngqīyī shàngwǔ	h. xīngqīsì yèlǐ	l. míngtiān xìawǔ
		m. míngtiān wǎnshàng

So, with merely **shíyī ge cí**, *(shr-yee)(guh) (tsr)* eleven (C) words, you can specify any day of the **xīngqī** *(sseeng-chee)* week and any time of the **tian**. *(tee-ahn)* day The words **"jīntian,"** *(jeen-tee-ahn)* today **"míngtian"** *(meeng-tee-ahn)* tomorrow and **"zúotian"** *(zwo-tee-ahn)* yesterday will be **hěn** *(huhn)* very important in making reservations and appointments, in getting **xìpiào** *(ssee-pee-ow)* theater tickets and for many other things you will want to do. Knowing the parts of the **tīan** will help you to understand the various forms of "good-bye" in the **Zhōnggúo hùa**. *(hwah)* language

see you tomorrow	=	*(meeng-tee-ahn)(jee-ahn)* **míngtian jìan**
see you in the afternoon	=	*(ssee-ah-woo) (jee-ahn)* **xiàwǔ jìan**
see you in the evening	=	*(wahn-shahng) (jee-ahn)* **wǎnshàng jìan**
see you tomorrow afternoon	=	*(meeng-tee-ahn)(ssee-ah-woo)(jee-ahn)* **míngtian xìawǔ jìan**

_____

xìawǔ jìan

_____

_____

Take the next **sì ge** *(sr)* four (C) labels and stick them on the appropriate things in your **fángzi**. *(fahng-zr)* house

What about the bathroom mirror for **"míngtian jìan"**? Or a wall clock for **"xìawǔ jìan"**?

Remember that, in **Zhōnggúo,** *(jung-gwo)* people do not say "good morning," "good afternoon" or "good night." You may be greeted with **"Nǐ hǎo?"** *(nee) (how)* you well meaning "How are you?"

In **Zhōnggúo,** you are much more likely to hear a form of "good-bye" like **"zài jian,"** *(zi) (jee-ahn)* which means "See you again." If you really want to enjoy **Zhōnggúo,** *(jung-gwo)* learn the different forms of "good-bye"—you will hear them often.

You are about one-fourth of your way through **zhèi běn shū,** *(jay) (buhn) (shoo)* this (C) book and it is a good time to quickly review the **cí** you have learned before doing the crossword puzzle on the next page.

22

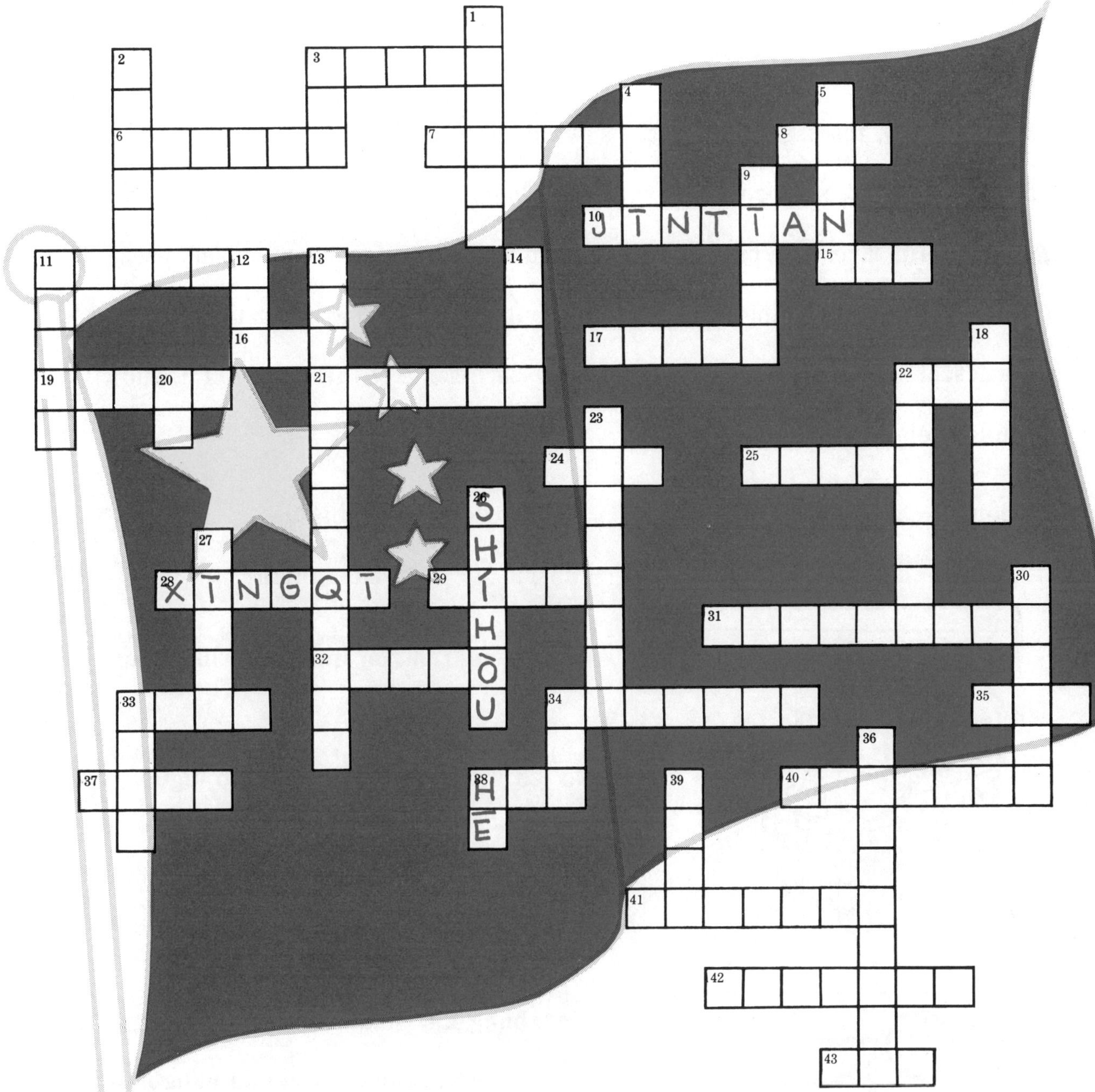
JĪNTIĀN
XĪNGQĪ
SHÍHÒU
HĒ

ACROSS

3. number
6. house
7. name
8. gray
10. today
11. hotel
15. dog
16. people
17. beer
19. woman
21. pen
22. cat
24. book
25. boat
28. week
29. carpet
31. bicycle
32. lavatory
33. red
34. garden
35. ball
37. salad
38. black
40. lamp
41. bank
42. brown
43. meat

DOWN

1. theater ticket
2. place
3. ten
4. chair
5. yellow
9. gasoline
11. two
12. where
13. bus
14. water
18. we
20. two
22. doorbell
23. window
26. time
27. egg
30. living room
33. flower
34. sea
36. banana
38. to drink
39. orange

Step 8

(lee) *(shahng)* *(wi)*
Lǐ, Shǎng, Wài
inside   on   outside

While in *(jung-gwo)* **Zhōngguó,** the use of prepositions (words like "in," "on," "through," and "next to") will allow you to be precise with a minimum amount of effort. Instead of having to point *(lee-oh)* **lìu** six times at a piece of jewelry you wish to buy, you can explain precisely which piece you want by saying **zài** *it is* behind, in front of, next to, or under the jewelry that the salesperson is starting to pick up. Let's learn some of these little **cí.** Study the examples below.

(tswong) **cóng** = from	*(pahng-bee-ahnr)* **pangbianr** = next to *by side*	*(ssee-ah-bee-ahnr)* **xiabianr** = under, below *under side*
(jeen) **jin** = into, in	**lǐ** = inside	*(shahng-bee-ahnr)* **shangbianr** = over *top side*

(nah) (guh) (nahn-ruhn)(zoh) (jeen)   (sseen) (lew-gwahn)
Nà ge nánrén zou jìn nà ge xīn lǘguǎn.
that (C) man enters into   new   hotel

(nah) (guh) (new-ruhn) (tswong)   (how) (lew-gwahn) (choo) (li)
Nà ge nǚrén cóng nà ge hǎo lǘguǎn chū lái.
that (C) woman from   good hotel   out come

(yee-shuhng)(zi)   (how)   (lee)
Nà ge yīshēng zài nà ge hǎo lǘguǎn lǐ.
doctor is   good hotel   inside

(nah) (jahng) (sseen) (hwar) (zi) (jwo-zr) (shahng-bee-ahnr)
Nà zhāng xīn hùar zài zhūozi shàngbīanr.
(C)   new picture is table over

(nah) (jahng)   (zi) (jung) (pahng-bee-ahnr)
Nà zhāng xīn hùar zài zhōng pángbīanr.
that (C)   new picture is clock next to

(kah-fay-suh) (jwo-zr)   (hwar) (ssee-ah-bee-ahnr)
Nà ge kāfēisè zhūozi zài hùar xīabīanr.
brown   table   is   picture under

(hway) (goh)   (jwo-zr) (pahng-bee-ahnr)
Nà ge hūi gǒu zài zhūozi pángbīanr.
gray   dog   table   next to

(lew) (jung)   (jwo-zr) (shahng-bee-ahnr)
Nà ge lü zhōng zài zhūozi shàngbīanr.
green clock   table   over

(lew) (jung)   (hwar) (pahng-bee-ahnr)
Nà ge lü zhōng zài hùar pangbīanr.
green clock   picture next to

☐ **cài** *(tsi)* . . . . vegetable
☐ **báicài** *(bi-tsi)* . . . . cabbage
☐ **bócài** *(bwo-tsi)* . . . . spinach
☐ **qíncài** *(cheen-tsi)* . . . . celery
☐ **shēngcài** *(shung-tsi)* . . . . lettuce

菜
cai

Fill in the blanks below with the correct preposition according to the **hùar** *(hwar)* on the
pictures

previous **ye.** *(yeh)*
page

Nà ge nánrén zǒu _____ **nà ge xīn lügǔan.**
(nahn-ruhn) (zoh) *(sseen) (lew-gwahn)*
that   man   enters   that   new   hotel

Nà ge hūi gǒu zài zhūozi _____.
(hway) (goh) (zi) (jwo-zr)
(C)   gray   dog   is   table

Nà ge lü zhōng zài zhūozi _____.
(lew) (jung) *(jwo-zr)*
that   green clock   table

Nà zhāng xīn hùar zài zhūozi _____.
(sseen) (hwar) (jwo-zr)
new   picture   is   table

Nà ge lü zhōng zài hùar _____.
(lew) (jung) (hwar)
green clock   picture

Nà ge yīshēng zài nà ge hǎo lügǔan
(yee-shuhng) *(how) (lew-gwahn)*
(C)   doctor   is   good   hotel

Nà zhāng kāfēisè zhūozi zài hùar _____.
(jahng) (kah-fay-suh) (jwo-zr) (hwar)
(C)   brown   table   is   picture

_____.

Nà zhāng xīn hùar zài zhōng _____.
new   picture   is

Xìanzài, answer these questions based on the **hùar** on the previous **yè.** Notice that the
(ssee-ahn-zi)
now   pictures   page

word **"ma"** is used at the end of yes-no questions.
(mah)

Yīshēng zài nǎr? _____
(yee-shuhng) (zi) (nahr)
doctor   is   where

Gǒu zài nǎr? *Nà ge gǒu zài zhūozi pángbīanr.*
(goh) (zi) (nahr)
dog   is   where

Zhūozi zài nǎr? _____
(jwo-zr) (nahr)
table   is   where

Hùar zài nǎr? _____
(hwar) (nahr)
picture   is   where

Nà ge nǔrén zài zùo shénme? _____
(new-ruhn) (zwo) (shun-muh)
that   woman   is   doing   what

Nà ge nánrén zài zùo shénme? _____
(nahn-ruhn) (zwo)
that   man   is   doing   what

Zhōng shì lüde ma? _____
(jung) (shr) (lew-duh) (mah)
clock   is   green

Gǒu shì hūide ma? _____
(goh) (hway-duh) (mah)
dog   is   gray

☐ **càidān** *(tsi-dahn)* . . . . menu   _____
☐ **càiyáo** *(tsi-yow)* . . . . food eaten with rice   _____
☐ **càiyóu** *(tsi-yoh)* . . . . cabbage oil   菜   _____
☐ **càiyúan** *(tsi-yew-ahn)* . . . . vegetable garden   _____
☐ **càizǐr** *(tsi-zrr)* . . . . vegetable seeds   *cai*   _____

25

(ssee-ahn-zi)
Xiànzài for some more practice with *(jung-wuhn)* **Zhōngwén** prepositions.
now

(shahng) **shàng**	= on top of (horizontal surface), on (vertical surface)
(chee-ahn-bee-ahnr) **qíanbīanr** front side	= in front of
(hoh-bee-ahnr) **hòubīanr** rear side	= behind

(shway)   *(jwo-zr)*   *(shahng)*
Nà bēi shuǐ zài zhūozi shàng.
that glass water is table on

Nà bēi shuǐ zài zhūozi _shàng_ .

(chee-ahng)
Nà zhāng kāfēisède hùar zài qíang shàng.
that (C) brown picture is wall on

(chee-ahng)
Nà zhāng kāfēisède hùar zài qíang _____

(hwahng) *(dung)* *(jwo-zr)* *(hoh-bee-ahnr)*
Nà ge húang dēng zài zhūozi hòubīanr.
that (C) yellow lamp table behind

Nà ge húang dēng zài zhūozi _____.

(chwahng) *(chee-ahn-bee-ahnr)*
Nà ge kāfēisè zhūozi zài chúang qíanbīanr.
that (C) brown table bed in front of

Nà ge kāfēisè zhūozi zài chúang _____.

(hwah) *(chwahng)*
Nà ge hūa   chúang zài kāfēisè zhūozi
that (C) multi-colored bed brown table

Nà ge hūa chúang zài kāfēisè zhūozi ____

(hoh-bee-ahnr)
hòubīanr.
behind

_____.

Answer the following *(wuhn-tee)* **wèntí,** based on the *(hwar)* **hùar,** by filling in the blanks with the correct
questions   pictures
prepositions from those you have just learned.

(nah) *(buhn)* *(hohng)* *(shoo)* *(zi)* *(nahr)*
Nà bĕn hóng shū zài năr?
that (C) red book is where

Nà bĕn hóng shū zài kāfēisè zhūozi ——————.
brown   table

(lahn) *(goong-goong-chee-chuh)*
Lán gōnggòngqìchē zài năr?
blue bus is where

Lán gōnggòngqìchē zài *(hway)* **hūi** *(lew-gwahn)* **lǚgǔan** ——————.
gray   hotel

☐ **shí** *(shr)*	to eat		_____
☐ **shíwù** *(shr-woo)*	food		_____
☐ **shípǔ** *(shr-poo)*	cookbook, recipes	食	_____
☐ **shíyù** *(shr-yew)*	appetite	*shi*	_____
☐ **shíliáng** *(shr-lee-ahng)*	foodstuff, grain		_____

(hway) (dee-ahn-hwah)   *(lew) (dee-tahn)*   *(hwar)*

Hūi dìanhùa zài năr? **Lü dìtăn zài nar?** **Hùar zài năr?**

gray   telephone   is   where   green   carpet   picture

(hway) (dee-ahn-hwah)   *(bi) (chee-ahng)*

Nà ge hūi dìanhùa zài bái qíang _____.

gray   telephone   white   wall

(hwah)

Nà ge hūi dìanhùa zài hŭa hùar _____.

gray   telephone   multi-colored   picture

(hay) (jwo-zr)

Nà ge hūi dìanhùa zài hēi zhūozi _____.

black   table

(lew) (dee-tahn)   *(hay)*

Nà ge lü dìtăn zài hēi zhūozi _____.

green   carpet   black   table

(bi) (chee-ahng)

Nà zhāng hùar zài bái qíang _*shàng*_____.

(C)   picture   white   wall

(ssee-ahn-zi)

Xìanzài fill in each blank on the **lüguăn** below with the best preposition. The correct

now   hotel

(zi)   *(jay) (yeh)*

answers **zài** the bottom of **zhèi yè.** Have fun.

are at   this   page

旅馆

lüguăn

1._____

10. _*lĭ*_____

2._____

3._____

9._____

4._____

5._____

8._____

6._____

7._____

Step 9

(yee-yew-eh) *(ur-yew-eh)* *(sahn-yew-eh)*
Yīyùe, Èryùe, Sānyùe
January   February   March

(see-yew-eh) *(lee-oh-yew-eh)* *(jee-oh-yew-eh)* *(shr-yee-yew-eh)* *(doh)* *(yoh)* *(sahn-shr)* *(tee-ahn)*
Sìyùe,   **lìuyùe,**   **jǐuyùe,**   **shíyīyùe**   **dōu**   **yǒu**   **sānshí tīan.**
April   June   September   November   all   have   30   days

(sseeng-chee) *(ssee-ahn-zi)*
Sound familiar? You have learned the days of **xīngqī**, so **xìanzài** is the time to learn the
   week   now

(yew-eh) *(nee-ahn)* *(tee-ahn-chee)*
yùe of the **nían** and all the different kinds of **tīanqì** that you may encounter on your
months   year   weather

(tee-ahn-chee) *(jung-wuhn)*
holiday. For example, you ask about the **tīanqì** in **Zhōngwén** a little differently than you
        weather

(yeeng-wuhn) *(jeen-tee-ahn)* *(tee-ahn-chee)* *(yahng)*
do in **Yīngwén** — "**Jīntīan tīanqì zěnme yàng?**" Practice all the possible answers
English   today   weather   how   kind

(wuhn-tee)
to this **wèntí** and then write the following answers in the blanks below.
question

(tee-ahn-chee)
Jīntīan tīanqì zěnme yàng?

(jeen-tee-ahn) *(ssee-ah-yew)*
Jīntīan xìayǔ _____
today   rains

(ssee-ah-ssee-yew-eh)
Jīntīan xìaxǔe _____
today   snows

(noo-ahn-huh)
Jīntīan nǔanhe _____
     warm

(lung)
Jīntīan lěng _____
     cold

(tee-ahn-chee) *(how)*
Jīntīan tīanqì hǎo _____
     weather   good

(tee-ahn-chee) *(boo-how)*
Jīntīan tīanqì bùhǎo _____
     weather   not good

(ruh)
Jīntīan rè _____
     hot

(ssee-ah-woo)
Jīntīan xìawù _____
     foggy

(tsr)
Xìanzài practice the **Zhōngwén cí** on the next **yè** aloud and then fill in the blanks with
           words   page

(meeng-zr) *(yew-eh)* *(tee-ahn-chee)*
the **míngzi** of the **yùe** and the appropriate **tīanqì** report. Notice that a number precedes
names   months   weather

(yew-eh) *(sahn-yew-eh)*
the word for month, **yùe**, in **Zhōngwén**. For example, **sānyùe** means third month, or March.

☐ **gúo** *(gwo)* . . . .   nation, state   _____
☐ **Fǎgúo** *(fah-gwo)* . . . .   France   _____
☐ **Měigúo** *(may-gwo)* . . . .   America   玉   _____
☐ **Yīnggúo** *(yeeng-gwo)* . . . .   England   *guo*   _____
☐ **Zhōnggúo** *(jung-gwo)* . . . .   China   _____

(yee-yew-eh) **yíyùe** _____ January	*(ssee-ah-ssee-yew-eh)* **Yíyùe xìaxǔe.** _____ snows
(ur-yew-eh) **èryùe** _____ February	*(yeh) (ssee-ah-ssee-yew-eh)* **Èryùe yě xìaxǔe.** _____ also snows
(sahn-yew-eh) **sānyùe** _____ March	*(ssee-ah-yew)* **Sānyùe xìayǔ.** _Sānyùe xìayǔ._ rains
(sr-yew-eh) **sìyùe** _____ April	*(yeh) (ssee-ah-yew)* **Sìyùe yě xìayǔ.** _____ also rains
(woo-yew-eh) **wǔyùe** _____ May	*(gwah-fung)* **Wǔyùe gūafēng.** _____ windy
(lee-oh-yew-eh) **lìuyùe** _____ June	*(yeh) (gwah-fung)* **Lìuyùe yě gūafēng.** _____ also windy
(chee-yew-eh) **qíyùe** _____ July	*(huhn) (noo-ahn-huh)* **Qíyùe hěn nǔanhe.** _____ very warm
(bah-yew-eh) **báyùe** _____ August	*(ruh)* **Báyùe hěn rè.** _____ very hot
(jee-oh-yew-eh) **jǐuyùe** _____ September	*(tee-ahn-chee) (how)* **Jǐuyùe tīanqì hǎo.** _____ weather good
(shr-yew-eh) **shíyùe** _____ October	*(chahng-chahng) (ssee-ah-woo)* **Shíyùe chángcháng xìawù.** _____ often foggy
(shr-yee-yew-eh) **shíyīyùe** _____ November	*(huhn) (lung)* **Shíyīyùe hěn lěng.** _____ very cold
(shr-ur-yew-eh) **shíèryùe** _____ December	*(tee-ahn-chee) (boo-how)* **Shíèryùe tīanqì hěn bùhǎo.** _____ weather very not good

(ssee-ahn-zi)   *(wuhn-tee)*
Xìanzài answer the following **wèntí** based on the **hùar** to the right.
now   questions   pictures

(ur-yew-eh)   *(yahng)*
Èryùe tīanqì zěnme yàng? _____
February   weather   how   kind

(sr-yew-eh)   *(yahng)*
Sìyùe tīanqì zěnme yàng? _____
April   how   kind

(woo-yew-eh)
Wǔyùe tīanqì zěnme yàng? _____
May   kind

(bah-yew-eh)
Báyùe tīanqì zěnme yàng? _____
August

(how) (boo-how)
Tīanqì hǎo bùhǎo? _____
weather   good   not good

☐ **gúodù** *(gwo-doo)* . . . . country
☐ **gúogē** *(gwo-guh)* . . . . national anthem
☐ **gúohùi** *(gwo-hway)* . . . . parliament
☐ **gúojí** *(gwo-jee)* . . . . nationality
☐ **gúomín** *(gwo-meen)* . . . . people of a country   *guo*

29

Xìanzài for the seasons of the **nían** . . .
now   *year*

(dwong-tee-ahn)
dōngtian
winter

(choon-tee-ahn)
chūntian
spring

(ssee-tee-ahn)
xìatian
summer

(chee-oh-tee-ahn)
qiutian
autumn

dōngtian

Dōngtian lěng.
winter   cold
(lung)

Chūntian chángcháng
spring   often
(chahng-chahng)
(ssee-ah-yew)
xìayǔ.
rains

Xìatian rè.
summer   hot
(ruh)

Qiutian gūafēng.
autumn   windy
(gwah-fung)

At this point, it is a good time to familiarize yourself with **Zhōnggúo qìwěn.** *(chee-wuhn)* temperatures

Carefully read the typical **tīanqì** *(tee-ahn-chee)* weather forecasts below and study the thermometer because

temperatures in **Zhōnggúo** are calculated on the basis of Centigrade (not Fahrenheit).

húashì *(hwah-shr)*
Fahrenheit

shēshì *(shuh-shr)*
Centigrade

húashì	shēshì
212° F ——	100° C
98.6° F ——	37° C
68° F ——	20° C
32° F ——	0° C
0° F ——	-17.8° C
-10° F ——	-23.3° C

(shway) (ki)
shǔi kāi
water   boils

(jung-chahng) *(tee-wuhn)*
zhengcháng tǐwěn
normal   body temperature

(shway) (beeng) (dee-ahn)
shǔi bīng dǐan
water   freezing   point

(yahn) (shway) (beeng) (dee-ahn)
yán shǔi bīng dǐan
salt   water   freezing   point

(sahn-yew-eh) *(ur-shr)* *(sseeng-chee-yee)*
Sānyùe èrshí, xīngqīyī tīanqì
March   20   Monday   weather

(lung) *(gwah-fung)*
lěng, gūafēng
cold   windy
(chee-wuhn) *(doo)*
qìwěn 5 dù
temperature   degrees

(chee-yew-eh) *(shr-bah)* *(sseeng-chee-sahn)*
Qíyùe shíbā, xīngqīsān tīanqì
July   18   Wednesday   weather

(noo-ahn) *(cheeng)*
nǔan, qíng
warm   fine
(chee-wuhn) *(doo)*
qìwěn 20 dù
temperature   degrees

guo

(jee-ah)
Jīa
home

In **Zhōngguó,** not just the parents, but also the grandparents, aunts, uncles and cousins are all considered as close family, so let's take a look at the **cí** for them. Study the family tree below and then write out the **xīn cí** in the blanks that follow. Notice that, in **Zhōngguó,** the family name comes first, and the given name (or what we, in **Měiguó,** think of as the first name) follows.

(sseen) — over xīn (new)

(may-gwo) — over Měiguó (America)

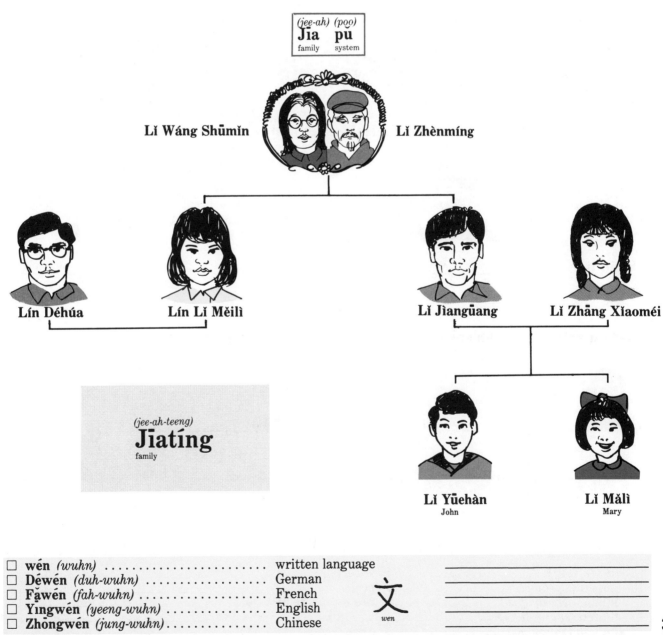

(jee-ah) (poo)
Jīa pǔ
family system

Lǐ Wáng Shūmǐn   Lǐ Zhènmíng

Lín Déhúa   Lín Lǐ Měilì   Lǐ Jiāngūang   Lǐ Zhāng Xǐaoméi

(jee-ah-teeng)
Jīatíng
family

Lǐ Yūehàn   Lǐ Mǎlì
John   Mary

☐ **wén** *(wuhn)*	written language	文	_____
☐ **Déwén** *(duh-wuhn)*	German	*wen*	_____
☐ **Fǎwén** *(fah-wuhn)*	French		_____
☐ **Yīngwén** *(yeeng-wuhn)*	English		_____
☐ **Zhōngwén** *(jung-wuhn)*	Chinese		_____

(zoo-foo-moo)
zǔfùmǔ
grandparents

(foo-moo)
fùmǔ
parents

(zoo-foo)
zǔfù _____
grandfather

(foo-cheen)
fùqīn _____
father

(zoo-moo)
zǔmǔ _____
grandmother

(moo-cheen)
mǔqīn _____
mother

(ssee-ow-hir)
xǐaoháir
children

(cheen-chee)
qīnqi
relatives

(ur-zr)
érzi _____
son

(shoo-shoo)
shūshu _____
uncle

(new-ur)
nǚ'er _____
daughter

(goo-goo)
gūgu _____
aunt

(yr-zr) *(new-ur)* *(guh-guh)* *(may-may)*
Érzi and **nǚ'er** are also **gēge** and **mèimei.**
son   daughter   older brother   younger sister

Let's learn **zěnme** to identify family members by **míngzi.** Study the following examples.
how   *(meeng-zr)* name

(foo-cheen) (jee-ow)
Fùqīn jìao shénme?
father   called   what

Fùqīn jìao _____.

(moo-cheen) (jee-ow)
Mǔqīn jìao shénme?
mother   called   what

Mǔqīn jìao _____.

Xìanzài you fill in the blanks, based on the **hùar,** in the same manner.
now   picture

_____ *(jee-ow)* **jìao shénme ?**
called   what

_____ **jìao** _____.

_____ *(jee-ow)* **jìao shénme ?**
called   what

_____ **jìao** *Mǎlì* .

- ☐ **shuǐ** *(shway)* . . . . water _____
- ☐ **shuǐchí** *(shway-chr)* . . . . pool _____
- ☐ **shuǐdào** *(shway-dow)* . . . . rice (in the field) _____
- ☐ **shuǐfèn** *(shway-fuhn)* . . . . moisture _____
- ☐ **shuǐgōu** *(shway-goh)* . . . . drain _____

水
shui

(choo-fahng)
Chúfáng
kitchen

Study all these *(hwar)* **hùar** and then practice
pictures

saying and writing out the *(tsr)* **cí.**
words

(juh) *(shr)* *(choo-fahng)*
Zhè shì chúfáng.
this   is   kitchen

(beeng-ssee-ahng)
bīngxīang
refrigerator

_____

(loo-zr)
lúzi
stove

lúzi

_____

(jee-oh)
jǐu
wine

_____

(pee-jee-oh)
píjǐu
beer

_____

(nee-oh-ni)
níunǎi
milk

_____

(hwahng-yoh)
húangyóu
butter

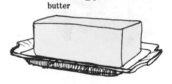

_____

Answer the *(wuhn-tee)* **wèntí** aloud.
questions

(pee-jee-oh) *(zi)* *(nahr)*
Píjǐu   zài nǎr? . . . .
beer   is   where

(nee-oh-ni)
Níunǎi zài nǎr?
milk

(jee-oh)
Jǐu zài nǎr?
wine

(pee-jee-oh) *(zi)* *(beeng-ssee-ahng)* *(lee)*
Píjǐu   zài   bīngxīang   lǐ.
beer   is   refrigerator   inside

(hwahng-yoh)
Húangyóu zài nǎr?
butter

☐ **shǔikù** *(shway-koo)* . . . . reservoir
☐ **shǔishǒu** *(shway-shoh)* . . . . sailor
☐ **shǔiyù** *(shway-yew)* . . . . body of water
☐ **shǔizāi** *(shway-zi)* . . . . flood
☐ **shǔibà** *(shway-bah)* . . . . dam

shui

_____
_____
_____
_____
_____

33

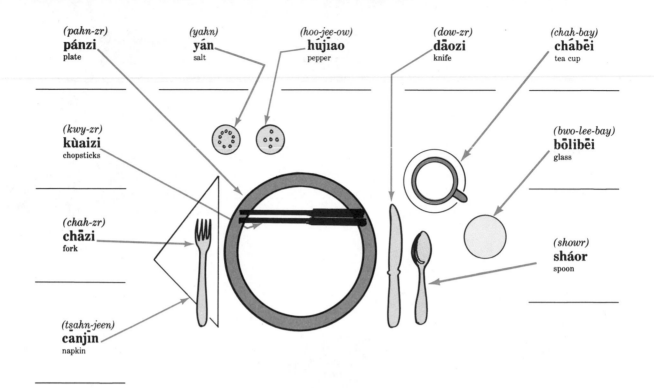

(pahn-zr) **pánzi** plate

(yán) **yán** salt

(hoo-jee-ow) **hújiao** pepper

(dow-zr) **dāozi** knife

(chah-bay) **chábēi** tea cup

(kwy-zr) **kùaizi** chopsticks

(bwo-lee-bay) **bōlibēi** glass

(chah-zr) **chāzi** fork

(showr) **sháor** spoon

(tsahn-jeen) **canjin** napkin

(gway-zr) **gùizi** cupboard

(mee-ahn-bow) **mìanbāo** bread

(chah) **chá** tea

(kah-fay) **kāfēi** coffee

chá

(mee-ahn-bow) (zi) (nahr)
Mìanbāo zài nǎr? **Mìanbāo zài gùizi** *(gway-zr) (lee)* **lǐ.** *(shway)* **Shǔi zài nǎr?** *(jyew-zr-shway)* **Júzishǔi zài nǎr?** *(ssee-ahn-zi)* **Xìanzài**
bread is where cupboard inside water orange juice

(dah-ki)
dǎkāi your **shū** with the labels and remove the next 22 labels. Proceed to label all
open

(dwong-ssee) *(choo-fahng)*
these **dōngxi** in your **chúfáng.** Do not forget to use every opportunity to say these
things kitchen

(juh) (huhn) (jwong-yow)
cí out loud. **Zhè hěn zhòngyào.**
this very important

□ **bīng** *(beeng)* . . . . ice
□ **bīngbáo** *(beeng-bow)* . . . . hail
□ **bīngdǐan** *(beeng-dee-ahn)*. . . . . freezing point
□ **bīnglěng** *(beeng-lung)* . . . . ice cold
□ **bīngqílín** *(beeng-chee-leen)* . . . . ice cream

氷
bing

(zwong-jee-ow)
Zōngjìao
religion

In **Zhōngguó,** a person's *(zwong-jee-ow)* **zōngjìao** *(peeng-chahng)* **píngcháng** *(shr)* **shì** one of the following.
religion   usually   is

1. *(jee-doo-jee-ow)* **jídǔjìao**   *jídūjìao*
Protestant

2. *(tee-ahn-joo-jee-ow)* **tīanzhǔjìao** _____
Catholic

3. *(hway-jee-ow)* **húijìao** _____
Moslem

4. *(fwo-jee-ow)* **fójìao** _____
Buddhist

This is a temple in **Zhōngguó.**

You will see several *(jwahng-yahn-duh)* **zhǔangyánde** temples like
magnificent

this on your visit. Occasionally, for special

events or for special visitors, religious

services are held in some of the temples.

(ssee-ahn-zi) **Xìanzài** let's learn how to say "I am" in *(jung-wuhn)* **Zhōngwén:**

I am =	*(wo) (shr)* **wǒ shì**
I am (in, on, at) =	*(wo) (zi)* **wǒ zài**

Practice saying **"wo shì"** *(wo) (shr)* and **"wo zài"** *(wo) (zi)* with the following **cí.** *(ssee-ahn-zi)* **Xìanzài** write out each

sentence for more practice.

(wo) (shr) (tee-ahn-joo-jee-ow) (too)
Wǒ shì tīanzhǔjìao tú. _____
I   am   Catholic   disciple

(wo) (shr) (jee-doo-jee-ow) (too)
Wǒ shì jídǔjìao tú. _____
I   am   Protestant   disciple

(hway-jee-ow) (too)
Wǒ shì húijìao tú. _____
Moslem

(fwo-jee-ow) (too)
Wǒ shì fójìao tú. _____
Buddhist

(oh-joh)
Wǒ zài Ōuzhōu.   *Wǒ zài Ōuzhōu*
am in Europe

(jung-gwo)
Wǒ zài Zhōngguó. _____
am in China

☐ **bīngshān** *(beeng-shahn)*	iceberg	
☐ **bīngshūang** *(beeng-shwahng)*	frost	冰 _____
☐ **bīngtáng** *(beeng-tahng)*	rock candy	_____
☐ **bīngxiang** *(beeng-ssee-ahng)*	refrigerator	*bing* _____
☐ **bīngzhù** *(beeng-joo)*	icicle	_____

35

(wo) (zi) (yeen-hahng) (lee)
Wǒ zài yínháng lǐ. _____
I   am   bank   inside

(wo) (zi) (choo-fahng) (lee)
Wǒ zài chúfáng lǐ. _____
I   am   kitchen   inside

(wo) (shr) (moo-cheen)
Wǒ shì mǔqin. _____
I   am   mother

(wo) (shr) (foo-cheen)
Wǒ shì fùqin. _____
I   am   father

(lew-gwahn) (lee)
Wǒ zài lǚguǎn lǐ. _____
hotel   inside

(fahn-gwahnr) (lee)
Wǒ zài fànguǎnr lǐ. _____
restaurant   inside

(zoo-moo)
Wǒ shì zǔmǔ. _____
grandmother

(zoo-foo)
Wǒ shì zǔfù. _____
grandfather

(ssee-ahn-zi)
Xìanzài identify all the **rén** in the **hùar** below by writing the **zhěngqùede** **Zhōngwén cí**
(ruhn)   *(hwar)*   *(jung-chyew-eh-duh)*
person   picture   correct   Chinese   word

(ruhn)   *(hwar)*
for each **rén** on the line with the corresponding number under the **hùar**.
person   picture

1. _____   2. _____

3. _____   4. _____

5. _____*shūshu*_____   6. _____

7. _____

☐ **fēi** *(fay)* . . . . to fly
☐ **fēijī** *(fay-jee)* . . . . airplane
☐ **fēijīchǎng** *(fay-jee-chahng)* . . . . airport
☐ **fēijīkù** *(fay-jee-koo)* . . . . hangar
☐ **fēiqín** *(fay-cheen)* . . . . bird

fei _____
_____
_____
_____

(ssee-yew-eh-ssee)
Xúexí
learn

You have already used the verbs **yǒu** *(yoh)*, **xiǎng** *(ssee-ahng)* **yào** *(yow)*, **zǒu** *(zoh)*, **lái** *(li)*, **shì** *(shr)* and **zùo** *(zwo)*. Although you
have   would like   walk   come   be   do

might be able to "get by" with these verbs, let's assume you want to do better than that.

First, a quick review.

In **Zhōngwén**, how do you say ☐ "I"? *wǒ* In **Zhōngwén**, how do you say ☐ "we"? _____

Compare **zhè** *(juh)* **liǎng** *(lee-ahng)* **ge** *(guh)* charts
these   two   (C)

hěn *(huhn)* carefully and **xúexí** *(ssee-yew-eh-ssee)*
very   learn

zhè *(juh)* **bá** *(bah)* **ge** *(guh)* **cí** *(tsr)* on the right.
these   eight   (C)   words

I = **wǒ** *(wo)*	
you = **nǐ** *(nee)*	
he = **tā** *(tah)*	
she = **tā** *(tah)*	
it = **tā** *(tah)*	

we = **wǒmen** *(wo-muhn)*	
you = **nǐmen** *(nee-muhn)*	
they = **tāmen** *(tah-muhn)*	

Xìanzài draw lines between the matching **Yīngwén** *(yeeng-wuhn)* and **Zhōngwén** *(jung-wuhn)* **cí** *(tsr)* below to see if you can
English   Chinese   words

keep these **cí** straight in your mind.
words

wǒmen	he
tā	I
wǒ	you
tā	it
nǐ	we
tā	they
tāmen	she

Xìanzài close this **shū** and write out both columns of the above practice on a piece of **zhǐ** *(jr)*.
paper

How did **nǐ** *(nee)* do? **Hǎo** *(how)*, or **bùhǎo** *(boo-how)*? **Mǎmǎhūhū** *(mah-mah-hoo-hoo)*? **Xìanzài** that **nǐ** *(nee)* know these **cí** *(tsr)*, **nǐ** *(nee)* can say
you   well   not well   so so   words

almost anything in **Zhōngwén** as long as you know the correct verb.

☐ **fēisù** *(fay-soo)*	quickly	
☐ **fēiwǔ** *(fay-woo)*	to flutter	
☐ **fēixíng** *(fay-sseeng)*	to soar	*fei*
☐ **fēixíngyúan** *(fay-sseeng-yew-ahn)*	pilot	
☐ **fēiyú** *(fay-yew)*	flying fish	

To demonstrate, let's take **lìu** *(lee-oh)* **ge** *(guh)* basic and practical verbs and see how easy verbs are.
six (C)

Write the verbs in the blanks below after **nǐ** have practiced saying them.

lái *(li)* = to come   **qù** *(chee-yew)* = to go   **xúexí** *(ssee-yew-eh-ssee)* = to learn

lái _____   _____   _____

xūyào *(ssee-yew-yow)* = to need   **yǒu** *(yoh)* = to have   **xiǎng yào** *(ssee-ahng) (yow)* = would like

_____   _____   _____

Study the following verb patterns carefully.

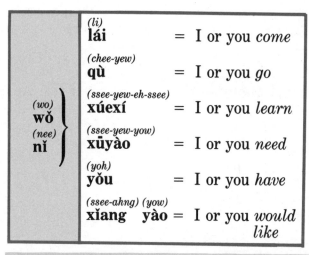

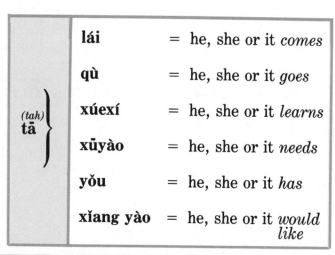

Note: • Unlike English, the same word is used for he, she and it: **tā.** *(tah)*

Notice that **wǒmen,** *(wo-muhn)* we **nǐmen** *(nee-muhn)* you and **tāmen** *(tah-muhn)* they use the same verb form as **wǒ,** *(wo)* I **nǐ** *(nee)* you and **tā.** *(tah)* he, she, it

wǒmen *(wo-muhn)*	**lái** *(li)* = we, you or they *come*	**xūyào** *(ssee-yew-yow)* = we, you or they *need*
nǐmen *(nee-muhn)*	**qù** *(chee-yew)* = we, you or they *go*	**yǒu** *(yoh)* = we, you or they *have*
tāmen *(tah-muhn)*	**xúexí** *(ssee-yew-eh-ssee)* = we, you or they *learn*	**xiǎng yào** *(ssee-ahng) (yow)* = we, you or they *would like*

☐ **shū** *(shoo)* .... book
☐ **shūbāo** *(shoo-bow)* .... bookbag
☐ **shūchú** *(shoo-choo)* .... bookcase
☐ **shūdìan** *(shoo-dee-ahn)* .... bookstore
☐ **shūfǎ** *(shoo-fah)* .... handwriting, calligraphy

书
shu

_____
_____
_____
_____
_____

- Regardless of the subject of the verb, in Chinese the same verb form is used.

    Verbs do not have different endings.

    ex. **wǒ yǒu** *(yoh)*   ex. **wǒ lái** *(li)*

    nǐ yǒu   **nǐ lái**

    tā yǒu   **tā lái**

    wǒmen yǒu   **wǒmen lái**

    nǐmen yǒu   **nǐmen lái**

    tāmen yǒu   **tāmen lái**

- "**men**" *(muhn)* is added to a word to indicate more than one person, as in **wǒmen**, *(wo-muhn)*
  we
  nǐmen *(nee-muhn)* and **tāmen**. *(tah-muhn)*
  you   they

In **Zhōngwén,** **dòngcí** *(dwong-tsr)* are easy to learn. Fill in the following blanks with the **dòngcí** *(dwong-tsr)*
verbs   verb
shown. Each time **nǐ** read the sentence, be sure to say it aloud. At the back of this

shū, nǐ will also find flash cards that will help **nǐ** to learn these new **dòngcí.** Cut them out,

carry them in your briefcase, purse, pocket or backpack, and review them whenever **nǐ**

have a free moment.

xúexí *(ssee-yew-eh-ssee)*
learn

Wǒ _____ **Zhōngwén.** *(wo)*
I

Nǐ _____ **Yīngwén.** *(nee)* *(yeeng-wuhn)*
you   English

Tā _____ **Zhōngwén.** *(tah)*
he, she, it

Wǒmen *xúexí* **Yīngwén.** *(wo-muhn)* *(yeeng-wuhn)*
we   English

Tāmen _____ **Zhōngwén.** *(tah-muhn)*
they

lái *(li)*
come

Wǒ _____ **Měiguó.** *(may-gwo)*
America

Nǐ *lái* **Dégúo.** *(duh-gwo)*
Germany

Tā _____ **Fǎguó.** *(fah-gwo)*
France

Wǒmen _____ **Yīnggúo.** *(yeeng-gwo)*
England

Tāmen _____ **Zhōnggúo.**

☐ **shūfáng** *(shoo-fahng)* . . . . study, den
☐ **shūjià** *(shoo-jee-ah)* . . . . bookshelf
☐ **shūpíng** *(shoo-peeng)* . . . . book review
☐ **shūqian** *(shoo-chee-ahn)* . . . . bookmark
☐ **shūzhuo** *(shoo-jwo)* . . . . desk

书
shu

_____
_____
_____

(chee-yew)
qù
go

(wo) **Wǒ** _____ **Dégúo.** *(duh-gwo)*
I / Germany

(nee) **Nǐ** _____ *qù* _____ **Fǎgúo.** *(fah-gwo)*
you / France

(tah) **Tā** _____ **Yìdàlì.** *(yee-dah-lee)*
he, she, it / Italy

(wo-muhn) **Wǒmen** _____ **Hélán.** *(huh-lahn)*
we / Netherlands

(tah-muhn) **Tāmen** _____ **Zhōnggúo.**
they

(ssee-yew-yow)
xūyào
need

(wo) **Wǒ** _____ **yì jīan wūzi.** *(yee) (jee-ahn) (woo-zr)*
one (C) room

(nee) **Nǐ** _____ **yì jīan wūzi.** *(yee) (jee-ahn) (woo-zr)*
one (C) room

Tā _____ *xūyào* _____ **yì jīan wūzi.**

Wǒmen _____ **yì jīan wūzi.**

Tāmen _____ **yì jīan wūzi.**

(yoh)
yǒu
have

(wo) **Wǒ** _____ *yǒu* _____ **wǔ yúan.** *(woo) (yew-ahn)*
five yuan

Nǐ _____ **lìu yúan.** *(lee-oh) (yew-ahn)*
six yuan

Tā _____ **bā yúan.** *(bah)*
eight yuan

Wǒmen _____ **shí yúan.** *(shr)*
ten yuan

Tāmen _____ **sān yúan.** *(sahn)*
three yuan

(ssee-ahng) (yow)
xǐang yào
would like

(wo) **Wǒ** _____ **yì bēi jǐu.** *(yee) (bay) (jee-oh)*
cup, glass wine

Nǐ _____ **yì bēi chá.** *(yee) (bay) (chah)*
cup tea

Tā _____ **yì bēi shǔi.** *(bay) (shway)*
glass water

Wǒmen _____ **yì bēi júzishǔi.** *(jyew-zr-shway)*
orange juice

Tāmen _____ *xǐang yào* _____ **yì bēi píjǐu.** *(pee-jee-oh)*
beer

(juhr) (yoh) (lee-oh) (guh) (dwong-tsr)
Zhèr yǒu lìu ge dòngcí.
here are six (C) verbs

(jee-ow) **jiao** = to be called

(my) **mǎi** = to buy

(shwo) **shūo** = to speak

_____

_____

_____

(joo) **zhù** = to live/reside

(jee-ow) **jiao** = to order

(teeng-lee-oh) **tínglíu** = to stay

_____

_____

_____

☐ **hǎi** *(hi)* . . . . sea
☐ **hǎi àn** *(hi) (ahn)* . . . . coast
☐ **hǎibīn** *(hi-been)* . . . . seashore
☐ **hǎigǎng** *(hi-gahng)* . . . . seaport, harbor
☐ **hǎi mían** *(hi) (mee-ahn)* . . . . sponge

海
hai

_____
_____
_____
_____
_____

Xìanzài fill in the following blanks with the verb. Be sure to say each sentence out loud until **nǐ** have it down pat!

(jee-ow)
jìao
be called

Wǒ *jìao* _____ *(yew-eh-hahn)* Yūehàn.
John

Nǐ _____ *(mah-lee)* Mǎlì.
Mary

Tā _____ Jìan.

Wǒmen _____ Yūehàn, Mǎlì hé Jìan. *(huh)* and

Tāmen _____ Yūehàn, Mǎlì hé Jìan. *(huh)* and

(shwo)
shūo
speak

Wǒ _____ Zhōngwén.

Nǐ *shūo* _____ *(fah-wuhn)* Fǎwén.
French

Tā _____ *(yeeng-wuhn)* Yīngwén.
English

Wǒmen _____ *(rr-wuhn)* Rìwén.
Japanese

Tāmen _____ *(duh-wuhn)* Déwén.
German

(jee-ow)
jìao
order

Wǒ _____ *(bay) (shway)* yì bēi shuǐ.
glass water

Nǐ _____ *(jee-oh)* yì bēi jǐu.
wine

Tā *jìao* _____ *(jyew-zr-shway)* yì bēi júzishuǐ.
orange juice

Wǒmen _____ yì bēi chá.

Tāmen _____ *(nee-oh-ni)* yì bēi níunǎi.
milk

(my)
mǎi
buy

Wǒ _____ *(yee)* yí lìang *(zr-sseeng-chuh)* zìxíngchē.
one (C) bicycle

Nǐ _____ yí ge *(guh) (sah-lah)* sālà.
(C) salad

Tā _____ *(jahng)* yì zhǎng *(hwar)* hùar.
(C) picture

Wǒmen *mǎi* _____ yí ge *(jung)* zhōng.
(C) clock

Tāmen _____ yi ge *(ti-dung)* táidēng.
(C) lamp

(joo)
zhù
live/reside

Wǒ _____ *(zi)* zài Zhōnggúo.
in

Nǐ _____ *(zi) (fah-gwo)* zài Fǎgúo.
in France

Tā _____ *(may-gwo)* zài Měigúo.
America

Wǒmen _____ *(oh-joh)* zài Ōuzhōu.
Europe

Tāmen *zhù* _____ *(duh-gwo)* zài Dégúo.
Germany

(teeng-lee-oh)
tínglíu
stay

Wǒ _____ *(woo) (tee-ahn)* wǔ tīan.
five days

Nǐ *tínglíu* _____ *(sahn) (tee-ahn)* sān tīan.
three days

Tā _____ *(lee-ahng)* lǐang tīan.
two

Wǒmen _____ *(lee-oh)* lìu tīan.
six

Tāmen _____ *(bah)* bā tīan.
eight

□ **hǎi tān** *(hi) (tahn)* .... beach
□ **hǎiwài** *(hi-wi)* .... overseas
□ **hǎi wān** *(hi) (wahn)* .... bay, gulf
□ **hǎi wèi** *(hi) (way)* .... seafood
□ **hǎi yáng** *(hi) (yahng)* .... ocean

海
hai

_____
_____
_____
_____
_____

Xìanzài see if **nǐ** can fill in the blanks below. The correct answers *(zi)* **zài** the bottom of
are at
(jay) *(yeh)*
zhèi yè.
this page

1. I speak Chinese. _____

2. He comes from America. _____

3. We learn Chinese. _____

4. They have 10 yuan. _____

5. She would like one glass of water. _____

6. We need one room. _____

7. I am called Mary. _____

8. I live in America. _____

9. You are buying one book. *Nǐ mǎi yì běn shū.*

10. He orders one glass of beer. _____

In the following steps, **nǐ** will be introduced to more and more **dòngcí,** *(dwong-tsr)* and **nǐ** should
verbs
drill them in exactly the same way as **nǐ** did in this section. Look up **xīn cí** *(sseen)* in your
new
(zr-dee-ahn)
zìdǐan and make up your own sentences using the same type of pattern. Remember, the
dictionary
more **nǐ** practice, the more enjoyable your trip will be. Good luck!

Be sure to check off your fun **cí** in the box provided as **nǐ** learn each one. ✔

(fuhn)
Fēn
minutes

Nǐ know **zěnme** *(zuhn-muh)* to tell the **tiān** of the **xīngqī** *(sseeng-chee)* and the **yuè** *(yew-eh)* of the **nían**, *(nee-ahn)* so **xiànzài** let's
how   days   week   months   year

learn to tell time. Punctuality **zài Zhōngguó hěn** *(zi)* **zhòngyào,** *(jwong-yow)* not to mention the need of
in   very   important

catching **huǒchē** *(hwo-chuh)* and arriving on time. **Zhèr** *(juhr)* **shì** *(shr)* the "basics." Notice that **le,** like
trains   here   are

ma, is often used to complete sentences and words in **Zhōngwén.**

What time is it? =	**Jǐ** *(jee)* **diǎn** *(dee-ahn)* **le?** *(luh)*
	how many o'clock
	Shénme *(shun-muh)* **shíhòu** *(shr-hoh)* **le?** *(luh)*
	what time

before	=	**chā** *(chah)*
after	=	**guò** *(gwo)*
half	=	**bàn** *(bahn)*

Wǔ diǎn. *(dee-ahn)*
five   o'clock

Sì diǎn bàn. *(dee-ahn)(bahn)*
four o'clock half

Sān diǎn.

Liǎng diǎn bàn. *(bahn)*
half

Bā diǎn èrshí fēn. *(fuhn)*
eight o'clock twenty minutes

OR

Bā diǎn guò èrshí fēn. *(gwo)(fuhn)*
after twenty minutes.

Qī diǎn sìshí fēn. *(dee-ahn)(fuhn)*
o'clock minutes

OR

Chā èrshí fēn bā diǎn. *(chah)*
before

Xiànzài fill in the blanks according to the **shíjiān** *(shr-jee-ahn)* indicated on the **zhōng.** *(jung)*
time

The answers **zài** below. Remember that **liǎng** *(lee-ahng)* means two in **Zhōngwén,** as does **èr.** *(ur)*
are

1. _____.

2. _____

3. _____

4. _____

5. _____.

6. _*sì diǎn*_____.

7. _____

8. _____

(juhr)
Zhěr are more time-telling **cí** to add to your **cí** power.
here

(yee) (kuh)
yí kè = one quarter

(chah) (kuh)
chà yí kè = one quarter before

(gwo) (kuh)
(gùo) yí kè = one quarter (after)

(dee-ahn) (kuh)
Liǎng diǎn yí kè.   OR   **Liǎng diǎn shíwǔ fēn.**
o'clock one quarter   minutes

Chà yí kè liǎng diǎn.   OR   **Yì diǎn sìshíwǔ fēn.**
         (kuh)

Xiànzài it is your turn.

 _____ .   _____ .

chà yí kě sān diǎn .   _____ .

(jwong-yow)   **(shoo-zr)**   **(wuhn-tee)**
See how **zhòngyào** learning **shùzì** is? **Xiànzài** answer the following **wèntí** based on the
         important   numbers   questions

zhōng below. The answers **zài** the bottom of **zhèi yè.**
                                                    (jay)
                                                    this

Jǐ diǎn le?

1. _____

2. _____

3. _____

4. _____

5. _____

6. _____

7. _____

ANSWERS

1. **qī diǎn bàn**
2. **liù diǎn**
3. **yī diǎn bàn**
4. **jiǔ diǎn guò èrshí (fēn)**
   (jiǔ diǎn èrshí fēn)

(qī diǎn sānshí fēn)

(yī diǎn sānshí fēn)

5. **bā diǎn**
6. **shíèr diǎn yí kè**
   (shíèr diǎn shíwǔ fēn)
7. **liǎng diǎn yí kè**
   (liǎng diǎn guò yí kè)

44

When **nǐ** answer a *(shr-jee-ahn)* **shíjiān** *(wuhn-tee)* **wèntí**, it is not necessary to say **fēn** *(fuhn)* after the

number of minutes.

火车 **6:00**

(hwo-chuh) **Huǒchē** shénme *(shr-hoh)* **shíhòu** *(li)* **lái?** ___Liù diǎn___.
train 火车 what   time   come

Xiànzài answer the following **wèntí** based on the **zhōng** below. Be sure to practice saying

each **wèntí** out loud several times.

(yeen-yew-eh) **Yīnyuè** *(hway)* **huì** shénme *(shr-hoh)* **shíhòu** *(ki-shr)* **kāishǐ?** _____.
music   concert what   time   start

(ssee-yew-ahn) **Xìyuàn** shénme shíhòu *(ki)* **kāi?** _____.
theater   open

(goong-goong-chee-chuh) **Gōnggòngqìchē** shénme shíhòu *(li)* **lái?** _____.
bus   come

(choo-zoo-chuh) **Chūzūchē** shénme shíhòu *(li)* **lái?** _____.
taxi   come

(fahn-gwahnr) **Fànguǎnr** shénme shíhòu *(ki)* **kāi?** _____.
restaurant   open

(fahn-gwahnr) **Fànguǎnr** shénme shíhòu *(gwahn-muhn)* **guānmén?** _____.
restaurant   close

Shàngwǔ bā *(dee-ahn)* **diǎn** *(jung-gwo-ruhn)* **Zhōngguórén** *(shwo)* **shuō,**
morning   o'clock   the Chinese person   says

"Nǐ hǎo ma, Wáng *(twong-jr)* **tóngzhì?"**
how are you   comrade

(ssee-ah-woo) **Xiàwǔ yì diǎn Zhōngguórén** *(shwo)* **shuō,**
afternoon   o'clock   says

"Chī *(chr)* **fàn** *(fahn)* **le ma,** *(twong-jr)* **tóngzhì?"**
have you eaten   comrade

Xiàwǔ sān diǎn Zhōngguórén *(chahng-chahng)* **chángcháng** *(shwo)* **shuō,**
afternoon   o'clock   often

"Jīntiān tiānqì hěn hǎo!"
today   weather   very   good

Wǎnshàng shí diǎn Zhōngguórén shuō,
evening   o'clock

"Míngtiān jiàn."
tomorrow   see you

☐ **fàn** *(fahn)* . . . . meal
☐ **fànguǎnr** *(fahn-gwahnr)* . . . . restaurant
☐ **wǎnfàn** *(wahn-fahn)* . . . . supper
☐ **wǔfàn** *(woo-fahn)* . . . . lunch
☐ **zǎofàn** *(zow-fahn)* . . . breakfast

饭
fan

_____
_____
_____
_____

45

Remember:

What time is it? =	*(shun-muh)* *(shr-hoh)* *(luh)* **Shénme shíhòu le?** **Jǐ dǐan le?** <small>how many o'clock</small>

When / at what time = *(shun-muh)* *(shr-hoh)*
shénme shíhòu

Can **nǐ** pronounce and understand

the following paragraph?

> *(hwo-chuh)*   *(shahng-hi)*
> **15:15 hǔochē cóng Shànghǎi lái.**
>
> *(ssee-ahn-zi)*   *(wahn)*
> **Xìanzǎi shì 15:20. Hǔochē wǎn le.**
> <small>late</small>
>
> **Jīntīan hǔochē 17:15 lái.**
>
> *(meeng-tee-ahn)*   *(zi)*
> **Míngtīan 15:15 hǔochē zài lái.**
> <small>again</small>

(juhr) *(yoh)*
Zher yǒu more practice exercises. Answer *(juh)* *(ssee-eh)* **zhè xīe wèntí** based on the *(shr-jee-ahn)* **shíjīan** given.
<small>here</small>   <small>these   several</small>

Jǐ dǐan le?

1. (10:30) *shí dǐan bàn* _____

2. (6:30) _____

3. (2:15) _____

4. (11:40) _____

5. (12:18) _____

6. (7:20) _____

7. (3:10) _____

8. (4:05) _____

9. (5:35) _____

10. (11:50) _____

☐ **fáng** *(fahng)*	room, apartment	
☐ **fángdōng** *(fahng-dwong)*	landlord	
☐ **fángkè** *(fahng-kuh)*	tenant	房
☐ **fángzi** *(fahng-zr)*	house	<small>fang</small>
☐ **wòfáng** *(wo-fahng)*	bedroom	

Zhèr yǒu yí ge *(juhr) (yoh)* quick quiz. Fill in the blanks with **zhèngquède shùzì** *(jung-chyew-eh-duh)*. The answers

here *is* *(C)* *correct*

zài xiàbīanr. *(ssee-bee-ahnr)*

under, below

1. **Yì fēn yǒu** *(fuhn)(yoh)* _____ **miao.** *(mee-ow)*

   minute has *(?)* *seconds*

2. **Yí ge zhōngtóu yǒu** *(jung-toh) (yoh)* _____ **fēn.** *(fuhn)*

   hour *has* *(?)* *minutes*

3. **Yì tīan yǒu** *(tee-ahn)* _____ **zhōngtóu.** *(jung-toh)*

   day *(?)* *hours*

4. **Yí ge xīngqī yǒu** *(sseeng-chee)* _____ *qī* _____ **tīan.** *(tee-ahn)*

   week *(?)* *days*

5. **Yí ge yùe yǒu** *(yew-eh)* _____ **tīan.** *(tee-ahn)*

   (C) month *(?)* *days*

6. **Yì nían yǒu** *(nee-ahn)* _____ **ge yùe.** *(yew-eh)*

   years *(?)* *(C) months*

7. **Yì nían yǒu** *(nee-ahn)* _____ **ge xīngqī.** *(sseeng-chee)*

   year *(?)* *(C) weeks*

8. **Yì nían yǒu** *(nee-ahn)* _____ **tīan.**

   year *(?)*

Zhèr is a sample **Zhōngguóde hǔochē shíjīan bǐao.** **Tèkùai shì tèbíe kùaide hǔochē.**

here *Chinese (hwo-chuh) (shr-jee-ahn) (bee-ow) (tuh-kwy) (tuh-bee-eh) (kwy-duh)*
train time schedule express special fast

Kùaichē bú tèbíe kùai, yěbú màn. Pǔtōngchē shì màn chē.

(kwy-chuh) (boo) (tuh-bee-eh) (kwy) (yeh-boo) (mahn) (poo-twong-chuh) (mahn) (chuh)
not specially fast neither slow ordinary train slow vehicle

Cóng Shànghǎi dào Nánjīng *(tswong) (dow)*			
from		*to*	
Kāi *(ki)*	**Hǔochē lèi** *(lay)*	**Dào** *(dow)*	**Fùjì** *(foo-jee)*
leave	*train type*	*arrive*	*remarks*
7:40	**Tèkùai**	8:30	🛏️ 🍴 🚃 ☎️
10:00	**Kùaichē**	11:10	🍴
12:15	**Kùaichē**	13:25	🍴 🚃
14:32	**Pǔtōngchē**	16:15	

ANSWERS

1. liùshí   2. liùshí   3. èrshísì   4. qī   5. sānshí/sānshíyī   6. shíèr   7. wǔshíèr   8. sānbǎi liùshíwǔ

47

Zhèr yǒu jǐ ge xīn dòngcí for Step 12.
(yoh) (jee) (sseen) (dwong-tsr)
here are some (C) new verbs

(shwo)
shūo = to say

(chr)
chī = to eat

(huh)
hē = to drink

_____   *chī* _____   _____

(shwo)
shūo
say

Wǒ jīntian ___*shūo*___.

Nǐ _____ "**hǎo!**" *(how)*

Tā jīntian _____ **hěn dūo.** *(huhn) (dwo)*
very much

Wǒmen _____ "**búyào.**" *(boo-yow)*
no thanks

Tāmen méi _____. *(may)*
didn't

(chr)
chī
eat

Wǒ _____ **shǔigǔo.** *(shway-gwo)*
fresh fruit

Nǐ _____ **zaofàn.** *(zow-fahn)*
breakfast

Tā _____ **yú.** *(tah)* *(yew)*
fish

Wǒmen _____ **ròu.** *(roh)*
meat

Tāmen _____ **jídàn.** *(jee-dahn)*
eggs

(huh)
hē
drink

Wǒ _____ **níunǎi.** *(nee-oh-ni)*
milk

Nǐ _____ **júzishǔi.** *(jyew-zr-shway)*
orange juice

Tā ___*hē*___ **jǐu.** *(jee-oh)*
wine

Wǒmen _____ **qìshǔi.** *(chee shway)*
soda pop

Tāmen _____ **chá.** *(chah)*
tea

Remember that "**c**" is pronounced like the "ts" in "its."

☐ **zhǐ** *(jr)* . . . . paper _____
☐ **bàozhǐ** *(bow-jr)* . . . . newspaper _____
☐ **shǒuzhǐ** *(shoh-jr)* . . . . toilet paper _____
☐ **zhǐbì** *(jr-bee)* . . . . paper currency _____
☐ **zìzhǐlǒu** *(zr-jr-loh)* . . . . wastebasket _____

纸
zhi

(hwar) **hūar**	*(shoo-fahng)* **shūfáng**	*(jee-oh)* **jǐu**	*(ssee-ah-woo)* *(jee-ahn)* **Xìawǔ jìan.**
(tee-ahn-hwah-bahn) **tīanhūabǎn**	*(dee-ssee-ah-shr)* **dìxìashì**	*(shr)* **shí**	*(wahn-shahng)* *(jee-ahn)* **Wǎnshàng jìan.**
(chee-ahng-jee-ow) **qíangjǐao**	*(chuh-fahng)* **chēfáng**	*(bi)* **bái**	*(meeng-tee-ahn)* *(ssee-ah-woo)* *(jee-ahn)* **Míngtīan xìawǔ jìan.**
(chwahng-hoo) **chūanghù**	*(chee-chuh)* **qìchē**	*(hay)* **hēi**	*(beeng-ssee-ahng)* **bīngxīang**
(dung) **dēng**	*(zr-sseeng-chuh)* **zìxíngchē**	*(hwahng)* **húang**	*(loo-zr)* **lúzi**
(ti-dung) **táidēng**	*(goh)* **gǒu**	*(hohng)* **hóng**	*(jee-oh)* **jǐu**
(shah-fah) **shāfā**	*(mow)* **māo**	*(lahn)* **lán**	*(pee-jee-oh)* **píjǐu**
(yee-zr) **yǐzi**	*(hwah-yew-ahn)* **hūayúan**	*(hway)* **hūi**	*(nee-oh-ni)* **níunǎi**
(dee-tahn) **dìtǎn**	*(sseen)* **xìn**	*(kah-fay-suh)* **kāfēisè**	*(hwahng-yoh)* **húangyóu**
(jwo-zr) **zhūozi**	*(yoh-twong)* **yóutǒng**	*(lew)* **lù**	*(pahn-zr)* **pánzi**
(muhn) **mén**	*(hwar)* **hūar**	*(fuhn)* **fěn**	*(dow-zr)* **dāozi**
(jung) **zhōng**	*(muhn-leeng)* **ménlíng**	*(hwah)* **hūa**	*(chah-zr)* **chāzi**
(chwahng-lee-ahn) **chūanglían**	*(yee)* **yī**	*(sseeng-chee-yee)* **xīngqīyī**	*(showr)* **sháor**
(chee-ahng) **qíang**	*(ur)* **èr**	*(sseeng-chee-ur)* **xīngqīèr**	*(kwy-zr)* **kùaizi**
(fahng-zr) **fángzi**	*(sahn)* **sān**	*(sseeng-chee-sahn)* **xīngqīsān**	*(tsahn-jeen)* **cānjīn**
(fahn-teeng) **fàntīng**	*(sr)* **sì**	*(sseeng-chee-sr)* **xīngqīsì**	*(chah-bay)* **chábēi**
(kuh-teeng) **kètīng**	*(woo)* **wǔ**	*(sseeng-chee-woo)* **xīngqīwǔ**	*(bwo-lee-bay)* **bōlibēi**
(wo-fahng) **wòfáng**	*(lee-oh)* **lìu**	*(sseeng-chee-lee-oh)* **xīngqīlìu**	*(yahn)* **yán**
(ssee-zow-fahng) **xǐzǎofáng**	*(chee)* **qī**	*(sseeng-chee-tee-ahn)* **xīngqītīan**	*(hoo-jee-ow)* **hújīao**
(choo-fahng) **chúfáng**	*(bah)* **bā**	*(meeng-tee-ahn)* *(jee-ahn)* **Míngtīan jìan.**	*(gway-zr)* **gùizi**

STICKY LABELS

This book has more than 150 labels for you to use as you learn new words. When you are introduced to a word, remove the corresponding label from these pages. Be sure to use each of these unique labels by adhering them to a picture, window, lamp or whatever object they refer to. The sticky labels make learning to speak Chinese much more fun and a lot easier than you ever expected.

For example, when you look in the mirror and see the label, say

(jeeng-zr)
"jìngzi."

Don't just say it once, say it again and again.

And once you label the refrigerator, you should never again open that door without saying

(beeng-ssee-ahng)
"bīngxīang."

By using the sticky labels, you not only learn new words but friends and family also learn along with you!

48a

(mee-ahn-bow)
mìanbāo

(chah)
chá

(kah-fay)
kāfēi

(shway)
shuǐ

(jyew-zr-shway)
júzishuǐ

(chwahng)
chúang

(bay)
bèi

(juhn-toh)
zhěntóu

(now-jung)
nàozhōng

(yee-choo)
yīchú

(ssee-shoh-chr)
xǐshǒuchí

(leen-yew)
línyù

(mah-twong)
mǎtǒng

(jeeng-zr)
jìngzi

(mow-jeen)
máojīn

(ssee-lee-ahn) *(mow-jeen)*
xǐlǐan máojīn

(ssee-ow) *(mow-jeen)*
xǐao máojīn

(ssee-zow) *(mow-jeen)*
xǐzǎo máojīn

(chee-ahn-bee)
qīanbǐ

(gahng-bee)
gāngbǐ

(jr)
zhǐ

(sseen)
xìn

(meeng-sseen-pee-ahn)
míngxìnpìan

(yoh-pee-ow)
yóupìao

(shoo)
shū

(zah-jr)
zázhì

(bow-jr)
bàozhǐ

(yahn-jeeng)
yǎnjìng

(dee-ahn-shr)
dìanshì

(zr-jr-loh)
zìzhǐlǒu

(hoo-jow)
hùzhào

(fay-jee-pee-ow)
fēijīpìao

(ssee-ahng-zr)
xīangzi

(pee-bow)
píbāo

(pee-jee-ah-zr)
píjīazi

(chee-ahn)
qían

(jow-ssee-ahng-jee)
zhàoxìangjī

(dee-pee-ahn)
dǐpìan

(yoh-yong-yee)
yóuyǒngyī

(lee-ahng-ssee-eh)
líangxíe

(fay-zow)
féizào

(yah-shwah)
yáshūa

(yah-gow)
yágāo

(gwah-lee-ahn-dow)
gūalǐandāo

(choo-hahn-jee)
chúhànjì

(shoo-zr)
shūzi

(wi-yee)
wàiyī

(yew-yee)
yǔyī

(sahn)
sǎn

(shoh-towr)
shǒutàor

(mow-zr)
màozi

(ssee-yew-eh-zr)
xūezi

(ssee-eh)
xíe

(wah-zr)
wàzi

(koo-wah)
kùwà

(shway-yee)
shùiyī

(shway-pow)
shùipáo

(wo) *(shr)* *(may-gwo-ruhn)*
Wǒ shì Měigúorén.

(wo) *(ssee-ahng)* *(yow)* *(ssee-yew-eh-ssee)* *(jung-wuhn)*
Wǒ xǐang yào xúexí Zhōngwén.

(wo) *(jee-ow)*
Wǒ jìao _____ .

(two-ssee-eh)
tūoxíe

(ssee-jwahng)
xīzhūang

(leeng-di)
lǐngdài

(shoh-jyew-ahnr)
shǒujùanr

(chun-yee)
chènyī

(shahng-yee)
shàngyī

(koo-zr)
kùzi

(lee-ahn-yee-chyewn)
líanyīqún

(chyewn-zr)
qúnzi

(mow-yee)
máoyī

(ssee-wong-jow)
xīongzhào

(chun-chyewn)
chènqún

(nay-koo)
nèikù

(nay-yee)
nèiyī

(dway-boo-chee)
dùibùqǐ

(cheeng)
qǐng

(ssee-eh-ssee-eh)
xìexie

PLUS . . .

Your book includes a number of other innovative features. At the back of the book, you'll find seven pages of flash cards. Cut them out and flip through them at least once a day.

On pages 113 and 114, you'll find a menu guide. Don't wait until your trip to use it. Clip it out and use it tonight at the dinner table. Refer to it to practice ordering your favorite foods.

By using the special features in this book, you will be speaking Chinese before you know it.

(yee-loo-peeng-ahn)
Yīlùpíngān!
safe and peaceful journey

(dwong) *(nahn)* *(ssee)* *(bay)*
Dōng - Nán, Xī - Běi
east   south   west   north

While in **Zhōngguó,** *(nee)* **nǐ** will probably use a *(dee-too)* **dìtú** to find your way around. Study the
you   map

direction words *(ssee-ah-bee-ahnr)* **xiàbianr** until **nǐ** are familiar with them and can recognize them on
below

your *(dee-too)* **dìtú** of **Zhōngguó.**
map

(dwong) **dōng** east	*(nahn)* **nán** south	*(ssee)* **xī** west	*(bay)* **běi** north

Notice on your *(dee-too)* **dìtú** how directions in **Zhōngguó** are given as eastsouth **dōngnán** and westnorth **xīběi**,
map

rather than southeast and northwest. Also notice how the direction words *(dwong)* **dōng,** *(nahn)* **nán,**
east   south

(ssee) **xī** and *(bay)* **běi** are used below with the words *(bee-ahnr)* **bianr,** meaning side, and *(fahng)* **fāng,** meaning direction.
west   north

(dwong-bee-ahnr) **dōngbianr**	=	East	_____
(nahn-bee-ahnr) **nánbianr**	=	South	_____
(ssee-bee-ahnr) **xībianr**	=	West	*xībianr*
(bay-bee-ahnr) **běibianr**	=	North	_____

(dwong-fahng) **dōngfāng**	=	eastern	_____
(nahn-fahng) **nánfāng**	=	southern	*nánfāng*
(ssee-fahng) **xifāng**	=	western	_____
(bay-fahng) **beifāng**	=	northern	_____

In **Zhōngwén,** *(ssee-yahng)* **xīyáng,** meaning west ocean, refers to any Western country, like the

United States, England or Germany. *(dwong-yahng)* **Dōngyáng,** meaning east ocean, refers to Japan.

But what about more basic directions such as "left," "right," "straight ahead" and "around

the corner"? Let's **xiànzài** learn these **cí.**
now

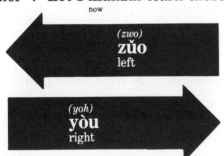

(zwo) **zuǒ** left

(yoh) **yòu** right

straight ahead	=	*(yee-jr)* *(zoh)* **yìzhí zǒu** straight walk
around the corner	=	*(gwy)* *(wahnr)* **guǎi wānr** turn corner
on the right side	=	*(zi)* *(yoh-bee-ahnr)* **zài yòubianr** right side
on the left side	=	*(zi)* *(zwo-bee-ahnr)* **zài zuǒbianr** left side

☐ **huǒ** *(hwo)* . . . . fire, flame   _____
☐ **gōuhuǒ** *(goh-hwo)* . . . . camp fire   _____
☐ **huǒchái** *(hwo-chi)* . . . . match   火   _____
☐ **huǒshān** *(hwo-shahn)* . . . . volcano   _____
☐ **huǒshí** *(hwo-shr)* . . . . flint   *huo*   _____

Just as in **Yīngwén,** (yeeng-wuhn) English **sān ge cí** (sahn) three (C) go a long way.

qǐng (cheeng)	= please	_____
xièxie (ssee-eh-ssee-eh)	= thank you	*xièxie*
duìbùqǐ (dway-boo-chee)	= excuse me	_____

Zhèr yǒu liǎng ge hěn diǎnxíngde duìhuà for someone who is trying to find something.
(juhr) (yoh) (huhn) (dee-ahn-sseeng-duh) (dway-hwah)
here are two (C) very typical conversations

Zhāng sān: **Duìbùqǐ. Běijīng Lǚguǎn zài nǎr?**
(dway-boo-chee) (bay-jeeng) (ley-gwahn) (zi) (nahr)
excuse me Beijing hotel is where

Lǐ sì: **Zài qiánbianrde jiàotáng, zuǒ zhuǎn. Zài zuǒbianr, nǐ kànjiàn yí ge**
(zi) (chee-ahn-bee-ahnr-duh) (jee-ow-tahng) (zwo) (juh-ahn) (zwo-bee-ahnr) (kahn-jee-ahn)
at front side church left turn at left side you see (C)
huáng fángzi nà shì Běijīng Lǚguǎn.
(hwahng)
yellow house that is

Zhāng sān: **Duìbùqǐ. Zhōngguó Bówùguǎn zài nǎr?**
(dway-boo-chee) (bwo-woo-gwahn)
excuse me museum

Lǐ sì: **Nǐ kànjiàn nà ge hóng qìchē ma? Zài qìchē qiánbianr, yòu zhuǎn. Nà jiē**
(kahn-jee-ahn) (hohng) (chee-chuh) (chee-ahn-bee-ahnr) (yoh) (juh-ahn) (jee-eh)
you see that (C) red car at car front side right turn that street
shàng, yǒu yí ge fànguǎnr. Bówùguǎn zài fànguǎnrde yòubianr.
(shahng) (yoh) (fahn-gwahnr) (bwo-woo-gwahn) (yoh-bee-ahnr)
on has one (C) restaurant museum is restaurant's right side

Are you lost? There is no need to be lost if **nǐ xuéxí le** the basic direction **cí.** Do
(ssee-yew-eh-ssee)
learned

not try to memorize these **duìhuà** because you will never be looking for precisely these
(dway-hwah)
conversations

places. One day you might need to ask for directions to "**Tàiyáng Fànguǎnr**"or
(ti-yahng) (fahn-gwahnr)
sun restaurant

"**Lìshǐ Bówùguǎn**" or "**Dàlù Lǚguǎn.**" Learn the key direction **cí** and be sure **nǐ** can
(lee-shr) (bwo-woo-gwahn) (dah-loo)
history museum mainland hotel

find your destination.

What if the person responding to your **wèntí** answers too quickly for you to understand
(wuhn-tee)
questions

the entire reply? If so, ask again, saying,

☐ **huā/huār** (hwah/hwar)	flower	_____
☐ **huāduǒ** (hwah-dwo)	blossom	_____
☐ **huāpíng** (hwah-peeng)	flower vase	花 _____
☐ **huāquān** (hwah-chee-yew-ahn)	wreath	*huā*
☐ **huāshù** (hwah-shoo)	bouquet	_____

(dway-boo-chee) (may-gwo-ruhn) (jee-oh)(hway)(shwo)(yee-dee-ahr)
Dùibùqǐ, wǒ shì Měigúorén. Wǒ jìu hùi shūo yìdǐar Zhōngwén.
excuse me   American   only can speak a little
(cheng)(mahn)(shwo) (cheng)(zi)(shwo)
Qǐng nǐ màn shūo. Qǐng zài shūo.
please slow speak please again speak

Xìanzài when the directions are repeated, **nǐ** will be able to understand them if **nǐ** learned
the key **cí** for directions. Quiz yourself by filling in the blanks below with the correct
Zhōngwén cí.

Jūehàn:
(dway-boo-chee) (hi-been)
Dùibùqǐ.   Hǎibīn Fàngǔanr zài nǎr?
excuse me   seashore restaurant

Mǎlì:
(zi)   (yoh-twong)   (joo-ahn)   (jee-eh)(shahng)(yoh)(huhn)
Zài _____ yóutǒng, _____ zhǔan. Nà jīe shàng yǒu hěn
at   front side   mailbox   right   turn that street on has very

(dwo)   (jahn)   (kahn-jee-ahn)
dǔo qìchē. Zài _____, gōnggòngqìchē zhàn, nǐ kànjìan yí ge
many cars at   left side   bus   stop you see   one (C)

(gow-duh)(bi) (fahng-zr)   (yoh) (hwah-yew-ahn)
hěn gāode bái fángzi. Fángzi _____ yǒu hūayúan.
very tall white house   front side   has garden

Nà shì Hǎibīn Fàngǔanr.
that is

(juhr) (yoh) (sr) (guh) (sseen) (dwong-tsr)
Zhèr yǒu sì ge xīn dòngcí.
here are four (C) new verbs
(jahn)
zhàn = to stand _____
(dwong)
dǒng = to understand   *dǒng, dǒng, dǒng*
(my)
mài = to sell _____
(zi)(shwo)
zài shūo = to repeat (say again) _____
again speak

□ **cháhūa** (chah-hwah)............... camellia
□ **júhūa** (jyew-hwah)............... chrysanthemum
□ **lánhūa** (lahn-hwah)............... orchid
□ **méihūa** (may-hwah)............... prune blossom
□ **xǔehūa** (ssee-yew-eh-hwah)...... snowflake

花
hua

51

As always, say each sentence out loud. Say each and every **cí** carefully, pronouncing
everything **nǐ** see.

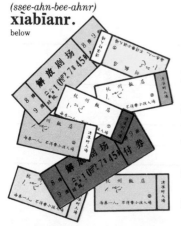

(jahn)
zhàn
stand

Wǒ _____ *zhàn_____*

(zi) (zwo-bee-ahnr)
zài zuǒbianr.
left side

Nǐ _____

(yoh-bee-ahnr)
zài yòubianr.
right side

Tā _____

(zi) (fahng-zr) (hoh-bee-ahnr)
zài fángzi hòubianr.
at   home   behind

Wǒmen _____

(chee-ahn-bee-ahnr)
zài fángzi qiánbianr.
in front of

Tāmen _____

(pahng-bee-ahnr)
zài fángzi pángbianr.
next to

(dwong)
dǒng
understand

Wǒ _____ **Zhōngwén.**

Nǐ _____ *dǒng_____*

(yeeng-wuhn)
Yīngwén.
English

Tā _____

(fah-wuhn)
Fǎwén.
French

Wǒmen _____

(duh-wuhn)
Déwén.
German

Tāmen _____

(rr-wuhn)
Rìwén.
Japanese

(my)
mài
sell

Wǒ _____

(chwahng)
chúang.
bed

Nǐ _____

(how) (yew)
hǎo yú.
good fish

Tā _____

(lew) (shahng-yee)
lǜ shàngyī.
green jacket

Wǒmen _____

(sseen) (dee-pee-ahn)
xīn dǐpian.
new   film

Tāmen _____

(ssee-pee-ow)
xìpiao.
theater tickets

(zi) (shwo)
zài shūo
repeat

Wǒ _____

(juh) (guh)
zhè ge cí.
this (C) word

Nǐ bú _____ .
not

Tā bú _____

(nah) (guh)
nà ge cí.
that (C)

Wǒmen _____ .

Tāmen bú _____ *zài shūo_____* .
(boo)
not

Xiànzài, see if **nǐ** can translate the following thoughts into **Zhōngwén.** The answers **zài**

(ssee-ahn-bee-ahnr)
xiàbianr.
below

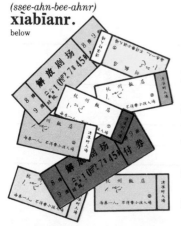

1. She repeats the word. _____

2. They sell theater tickets. *Tāmen mài xìpiao.*

3. He stands in front of the house. _____

4. We eat fish. _____

5. I speak Chinese. _____

6. I drink tea. _____

(shahng-bee-ahnr) *(ssee-ah-bee-ahnr)*
Shàngbianr, Xìabianr
over, above   under, below

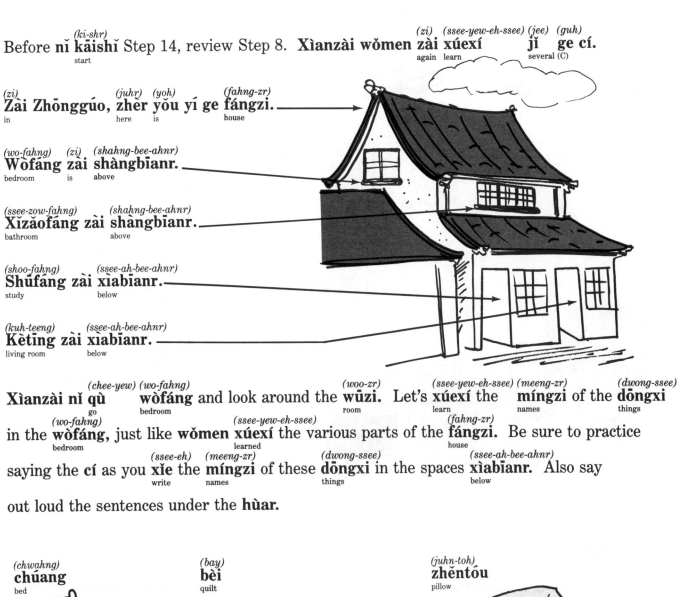

(ki-shr)
Before **nǐ kāishǐ** Step 14, review Step 8. **Xìanzài wǒmen zài xúexí jǐ ge cí.**
start
(zi) again learn *(ssee-yew-eh-ssee)* *(jee)* several (C) *(guh)*

(zi) *(juhr)* *(yoh)* *(fahng-zr)*
Zài Zhōngguó, zhèr yǒu yí ge fángzi.
in   here   is   house

(wo-fahng) *(zi)* *(shahng-bee-ahnr)*
Wòfáng zài shàngbianr.
bedroom   is   above

(ssee-zow-fahng) *(shahng-bee-ahnr)*
Xǐzǎofáng zài shàngbianr.
bathroom   above

(shoo-fahng) *(ssee-ah-bee-ahnr)*
Shūfáng zài xìabianr.
study   below

(kuh-teeng) *(ssee-ah-bee-ahnr)*
Kètīng zài xìabianr.
living room   below

(chee-yew) *(wo-fahng)* *(woo-zr)* *(ssee-yew-eh-ssee)* *(meeng-zr)* *(dwong-ssee)*
Xìanzài nǐ qù wòfáng and look around the **wūzi.** Let's **xúexí** the **míngzi** of the **dōngxi**
go   bedroom   room   learn   names   things

(wo-fahng) *(ssee-yew-eh-ssee)* *(fahng-zr)*
in the **wòfáng,** just like **wǒmen xúexí** the various parts of the **fángzi.** Be sure to practice
bedroom   learned   house

(ssee-eh) *(meeng-zr)* *(dwong-ssee)* *(ssee-ah-bee-ahnr)*
saying the **cí** as you **xiě** the **míngzi** of these **dōngxi** in the spaces **xìabianr.** Also say
write   names   things   below

out loud the sentences under the **hùar.**

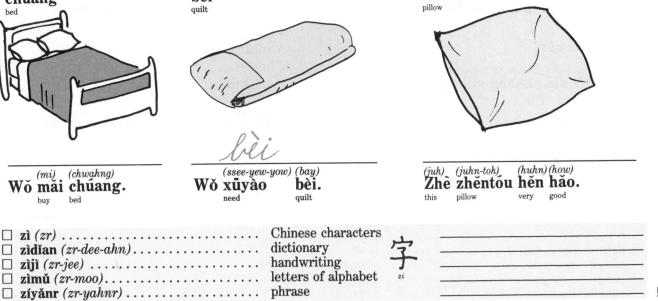

(chwahng)
chúang
bed

(bay)
bèi
quilt

(juhn-toh)
zhěntóu
pillow

bèi

(mi) *(chwahng)*
Wǒ mǎi chúang.
buy   bed

(ssee-yew-yow) *(bay)*
Wǒ xūyào bèi.
need   quilt

(juh) *(juhn-toh)* *(huhn)* *(how)*
Zhè zhěntóu hěn hǎo.
this   pillow   very   good

☐ **zì** *(zr)* . . . . Chinese characters
☐ **zìdiǎn** *(zr-dee-ahn)* . . . . dictionary
☐ **zìjì** *(zr-jee)* . . . . handwriting
☐ **zìmǔ** *(zr-moo)* . . . . letters of alphabet
☐ **zíyǎnr** *(zr-yahnr)* . . . . phrase

字
zi

(now-jung)
nàozhōng
alarm clock

(yee-choo)
yīchú
clothes closet

Remove the next **wǔ ge** stickers
(woo) (guh)
five (C)
and label these **dōngxi** in your
(dwong-ssee)
things
wòfáng.
(wo-fahng)
bedroom

(wo) (yoh) (yee) (guh)
Wǒ yǒu yí ge
I have one (C)
(now-jung)
nàozhōng.
alarm clock

(juh) (guh) (yee-choo) (zi)
Zhè ge yīchú zài
this (C) clothes closet is in
(wo-fahng)
wòfáng.
bedroom

Zài Zhōngguó, yí ge lǚguǎnde wòfáng.
in one (C) hotel's bedroom
(lew-gwahn-duh)
wò = to lie down (to sleep), so a sleeping room
(wo)

Study the following **wèntí** and their answers
(wuhn-tee)

based on the **zuǒbianrde huàr.**
(zwo-bee-ahnr-duh)
left

1. **Nàozhōng zài nǎr?**
(now-jung) (zi) (nahr)
alarm clock is where

  Nàozhōng zài zhuōzi shàng.
(jwo-zr) (shahng)
table on

2. **Bèi zài nǎr?**
(bay)
quilt

  Bèi zài chúang shàng.
(chwahng) (shahng)
bed on

3. **Yīchú zài nǎr?**
(yee-choo)
clothes closet

  Yīchú zài wòfáng.
(wo-fahng)
is in bedroom

4. **Zhěntóu zài nǎr?**
(juhn-toh) (zi) (nahr)
pillow is where

  Zhěntóu zài chúang shàng.
(chwahng) (shahng)
bed on

5. **Chúang zài nǎr?**
(chwahng)
bed

  Chúang zài wòfáng.
(wo-fahng)
is in bedroom

6. **Chúang dà ma? Chúang xǐao ma?**
(chwahng) (dah) (mah) (ssee-ow)
bed big small

  Chúang bú dà.
(boo) (dah)
not big

  Chúang xǐao.
(ssee-ow)
small

☐ **rén** *(ruhn)* . . . . person
☐ **nánrén** *(nahn-ruhn)* . . . . man
☐ **nǚrén** *(new-ruhn)* . . . . woman
☐ **réngé** *(ruhn-guh)* . . . . personality
☐ **rénkǒu** *(ruhn-koh)* . . . . population

ren

Xìanzài nǐ answer **wèntí** *(wuhn-tee)* based on the previous **hùar.**
questions

(now-jung)
Nàozhōng zài nǎr?
alarm clock

(chwahng)
Chúang zài nǎr?
bed

Let's move into the **xǐzǎofáng** *(ssee-zow-fahng)* and do the same thing.
bathroom

(ssee-shoh-chr)
xǐshǒuchí
washbasin

(leen-yew)
línyù
shower

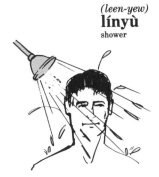

(mah-twong)
mǎtǒng
toilet

(ley-gwahn-duh) (woo-zr-lee) (yoh)
Lǚguande wūzilǐ yǒu
hotel   room   has
(ssee-shoh-chr)
yí ge xǐshǒuchí.
one (C) washbasin

(leen-yew) (boo) (zi)
Línyù bú zài lǚguǎn
shower   not in hotel
(woo-zr-lee)
wūzilǐ.
room

(mah-twong) (boo) (zi)
Mǎtǒng bú zài lǚguǎn
toilet   not   in hotel
(woo-zr-lee)   *(huh)*
wūzilǐ. Mǎtǒng hé línyù
room   toilet   and shower
(zi) (loh-dow)
zài lóudào.
are in corridor

(jeeng-zr)
jìngzi _____
mirror

(mow-jeen)
máojīn *máojīn* _____
towels

(ssee-lee-ahn)(mow-jeen)
xǐlian máojīn _____
washcloth

(ssee-ow) (mow-jeen)
xǐao máojīn _____
small/hand towel

(ssee-zow) (mow-jeen)
xǐzǎo máojīn _____
bath   towel

Do not forget to remove the **xìa bā ge** *(ssee-ah) (bah)* stickers and label these
next   eight   (C)

(dwong-ssee)   *(ssee-zow-fahng)*
dōngxi in your **xǐzǎofáng.**
things   bathroom

人
ren

55

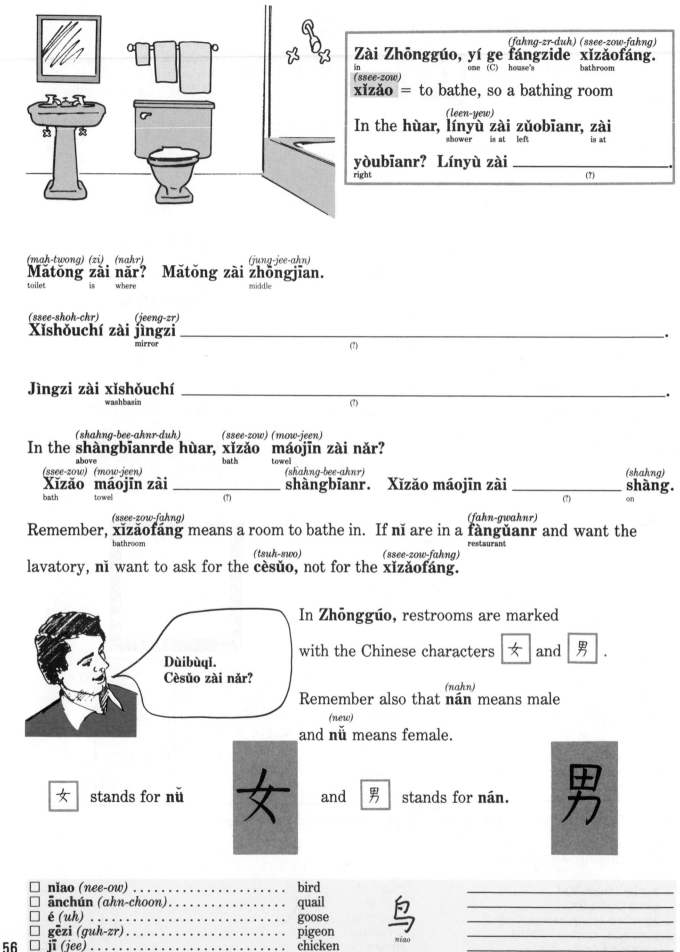

Zài Zhōngguó, yí ge fángzide xǐzǎofáng.
in one (C) house's bathroom
(fahng-zr-duh) (ssee-zow-fahng)

(ssee-zow)
xǐzǎo = to bathe, so a bathing room

In the **hùar, línyù zài zuǒbīanr, zài**
(leen-yew) shower is at left is at

yòubīanr? Línyù zài _____.
right (?)

Mǎtǒng zài nǎr? Mǎtǒng zài zhōngjīan.
(mah-twong) (zi) (nahr) *(jung-jee-ahn)*
toilet is where middle

Xǐshǒuchí zài jìngzi _____.
(ssee-shoh-chr) *(jeeng-zr)*
mirror (?)

Jìngzi zài xǐshǒuchí _____.
washbasin (?)

In the **shàngbīanrde hùar, xǐzǎo máojīn zài nǎr?**
(shahng-bee-ahnr-duh) *(ssee-zow) (mow-jeen)*
above bath towel

Xǐzǎo máojīn zài _____ **shàngbīanr. Xǐzǎo máojīn zài** _____ **shàng.**
(ssee-zow) (mow-jeen) (?) *(shahng-bee-ahnr)* (?) *(shahng)*
bath towel on

Remember, **xǐzǎofáng** means a room to bathe in. If **nǐ** are in a **fànguǎnr** and want the
(ssee-zow-fahng) bathroom *(fahn-gwahnr)* restaurant

lavatory, **nǐ** want to ask for the **cèsuǒ**, not for the **xǐzǎofáng**.
(tsuh-swo) *(ssee-zow-fahng)*

**Dùibùqǐ.
Cèsuǒ zài nǎr?**

In **Zhōngguó,** restrooms are marked

with the Chinese characters 女 and 男 .

Remember also that **nán** means male
(nahn)

and **nǚ** means female.
(new)

女 stands for **nǚ**   女   and 男 stands for **nán**.   男

- ☐ **nǐao** *(nee-ow)* . . . . bird
- ☐ **ānchún** *(ahn-choon)* . . . . quail
- ☐ **é** *(uh)* . . . . goose
- ☐ **gēzi** *(guh-zr)* . . . . pigeon
- ☐ **jī** *(jee)* . . . . chicken

鸟
niao

_____
_____
_____
_____
_____

Next stop — **shūfáng**, *(shoo-fahng)* specifically a **zhūozi** *(jwo-zr)* or **shūzhūo** *(shoo-jwo)* in the **shūfáng**. *(shoo-fahng)*
study table desk

Zhūozi *(jwo-zr)* **shàng** *(shahng)* **yǒu** *(yoh)* **shénme?** Let's identify the **dōngxi** *(dwong-ssee)* that one normally finds in the
table on has what things

shūfáng or strewn about the **fángzi.** *(fahng-zr)*
house

(chee-ahn-bee)
qiānbǐ
pencil

(gahng-bee)
gāngbǐ
pen

(jr)
zhǐ
paper

(sseen)
xìn
letter

gāngbǐ

(meeng-sseen-pee-ahn)
míngxìnpiàn
postcard

(yoh-pee-ow)
yóupiào
stamp

(shoo)
shū
book

(zah-jr)
zázhì
magazine

(bow-jr)
bàozhǐ
newspaper

(yahn-jeeng)
yǎnjìng
glasses

(dee-ahn-shr)
diànshì
television

(zr-jr-loh)
zìzhǐlǒu
wastebasket

☐ **máquè** *(mah-chyew-eh)*	sparrow		
☐ **wūyā** *(woo-yah)*	crow	鸟	
☐ **yā** *(yah)*	duck	*niao*	
☐ **yīng** *(yeeng)*	eagle		
☐ **zhīgēngniǎo** *(jr-gung-nee-ow)*	robin		

Xìanzài, label these **dōngxi** *(dwong-ssee)* in your **shūfáng** *(shoo-fahng)* with your stickers. Do not forget to say

these **cí** out loud whenever **nǐ xǐe** *(ssee-eh)* them, **nǐ** see them **hùoshì nǐ** *(hwo-shr)* apply the stickers.

Xìanzài identify the **dōngxi** in the **xìabīanrde hùar** *(ssee-ah-bee-ahnr-duh)* by filling in each blank with the

zhěngqùede Zhōngwén cí. *(jung-chyew-eh-duh)*
correct

1

4

5

6

2

7 CHINA DAILY

8

3 BEIJING REVIEW

9

10

1. _____
2. _____
3. _____
4. _____
5. _____
6. *míngxìnpìan*
7. _____
8. _____
9. _____
10. _____

Zhèr yǒu another **sì ge dòngcí.** *(juhr) (yoh) (dwong-tsr)*
here are   four (C) verbs

kànjìan *(kahn-jee-ahn)* = to see   **jì** *(jee)* = to send   **shùi** *(shway)* = to sleep   **zhǎo** *(jow)* = to look for

_____   _____   *shùi*   _____

Xìanzài fill in the blanks on the next page with the right **dòngcí.** *(dwong-tsr)* Practice saying
verb

the sentences out loud many times.

☐ **yī** *(yee)*	clothes	衣
☐ **chènyī** *(chun-yee)*	shirt, blouse	
☐ **dàyī** *(dah-yee)*	overcoat	
☐ **líanyīqún** *(lee-ahn-yee-chyewn)*	dress	
☐ **máoyī** *(mow-yee)*	sweater	*yī*

58

(kahn-jee-ahn)
kànjìan
see

Wǒ _kànjian_ **chúang.** *(chwahng)* bed

Nǐ _____ **běi.** *(bay)* quilt

Tā _____ **nàozhōng.** *(now-jung)* alarm clock

Wǒmen _____ **xǐshǒuchí.** *(ssee-shoh-chr)* washbasin

Tāmen _____ **línyù.** *(leen-yew)* shower

(shway)
shùi
sleep

Wǒ zài wòfáng _____ . *(wo-fahng)*
in   bedroom

Nǐ zài fǎngzilǐ _____ . *(fahng-zr-lee)*
house

Tā zài kètīng _shùi_____ . *(kuh-teeng)*
living room

Wǒmen zài shūfáng _____ . *(shoo-fahng)*
study

Tāmen zài lǚgǔan _____ . *(lew-gwahn)*

(jee)
jì
send

Wǒ _____ **xìn.** *(sseen)* letters

Nǐ _____ **míngxìnpìan.** *(meeng-sseen-pee-ahn)* postcards

Tā _____ **shū.** *(shoo)* books

Wǒmen _____ **míngxìnpìan.** *(meeng-sseen-pee-ahn)* postcards

Tāmen _____ **xìn.** *(sseen)* letters

(jow)
zhǎo
look for

Wǒ _____ **yóupìao.** *(yoh-pee-ow)* stamps

Nǐ _____ **zhǐ.** *(jr)* paper

Tā _____ **yǎnjìng.** *(yahn-jeeng)* glasses

Wǒmen _zhǎo_____ **gāngbǐ.** *(gahng-bee)* pen

Tāmen _____ **hùar.** *(hwar)* picture

Remember that the meanings of **Zhōngwén cí** vary depending on the tone used. Notice the differences in the meanings below, review the chart on page 2 and then practice using tones by saying each **cí** out loud.

(fahn)	*(jyew)*	*(tee)*
fān = to turn over	**jū** = colt	**tī** = ladder
fán = to bother	**jú** = department	**tí** = to lift
fǎn = to oppose	**jǔ** = to chew	**tǐ** = body
fàn = meal	**jù** = sentence	**tì** = to replace

☐ **nèiyī** *(nay-yee)* .... undershirt _____
☐ **shùiyī** *(shway-yee)* .... pajamas _____
☐ **shàngyī** *(shahng-yee)* .... jacket _____
☐ **yóuyǒngyī** *(yoh-yong-yee)* .... swimsuit _____
☐ **yǔyī** *(yew-yee)* .... raincoat _____

衣
yi

Step 15

Xìanzài nǐ know how to count, how to ask **wèntí,** how to use **dòngcí,** how to make
(dwong-tsr)
verbs

statements and how to describe something, be it the location of **yí ge lǚgǔan**
(lew-gwahn)
one (C) hotel

hùoshì yí ge fángzide yánsè. Xìanzài let's take the basics that **nǐ xúexíde**
(hwo-shr) *(fahng-zr-duh)* *(yahn-suh)*
or house's color
(ssee-yew-eh-ssee-duh)
have learned

and expand them in special areas that will be most helpful in your travels. What does

everyone do on a holiday? Send **míngxìnpìan,** of course. Let's learn exactly how
(meeng-sseen-pee-ahn)
postcards

Zhōnggúo yóujǔ works.
(yoh-jyew)
post office

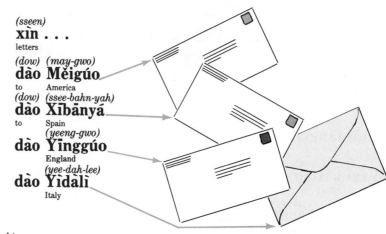

(sseen)
xìn . . .
letters
(dow) *(may-gwo)*
dào Měigúo
to America
(dow) *(ssee-bahn-yah)*
dào Xībǎnyá
to Spain
(yeeng-gwo)
dào Yīnggúo
England
(yee-dah-lee)
dào Yìdàlì
Italy

Zhōnggúo yóutǒngde yánsè shì lǜde.
(yoh-twong-duh) *(yahn-suh)* *(lew-duh)*
mailbox's color green

Zhèr shì the basic **yóuzhèng cí.** Be sure to practice them out loud and, **zài hùarde**
(yoh-jung)
postal
in

xìabǐanr, xǐe these **cí.**
(ssee-ah-bee-ahnr) *(ssee-eh)*
below write

(sseen)
xìn
letter

(meeng-sseen-pee-ahn)
míngxìnpian
postcard

(yoh-pee-ow)
yóupìao
stamp

(dee-ahn-bow)
dìanbào
telegram

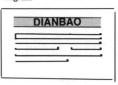

xìn _____ _____ _____ _____

☐ **xíe** *(ssee-eh)*	shoes		_____
☐ **bùxíe** *(boo-ssee-eh)*	cotton shoes		_____
☐ **píxíe** *(pee-ssee-eh)*	leather shoes	鞋	_____
☐ **qíuxíe** *(chee-oh-ssee-eh)*	sport shoes	*xie*	_____
☐ **tǔoxíe** *(two-ssee-eh)*	slippers		_____

(bow-gwo)
bāoguǒ
parcel

(yoh-twong)
yóutǒng
mailbox

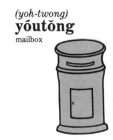

(hahng-kwong-sseen)
hángkōngxìn
air mail

HANGKONGXIN
AIRMAIL

(gway-ti)
guìtái
counter

_____

(dee-ahn-hwah) *(teeng)*
dìanhùa **tíng**
telephone booth

(dee-ahn-hwah)
dìanhùa
telephone

(yoh-jyew)
yóujú
post office

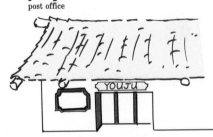

dìanhùa

_____

(yoh-jyew)
Zài Zhōngguó, the **yóujú** has everything. **Nǐ jì xìn** and **míngxìnpìan** and **dǎ**
in   post office   *(jee)* *(sseen)* *(meeng-sseen-pee-ahn)* *(dah)*
                                                     send letters   postcards   make
(dee-ahn-bow)   *(my)* *(yoh-pee-ow)*   *(yoh-jyew)*
dìanbào. Nǐ also **mǎi yóupìao** in the **yóujú.**
telegrams   buy stamps   post office

(ssee-yew-yow)   *(yoh-jyew)*   *(chahng-too)*
If **nǐ xūyào** to call home to **Měiguó,** this can be done at the **yóujú** and is called a **chángtú**
     need   post office   long-distance
(dee-ahn-hwah)   *(chee-yew)* *(yoh-jyew)*
dìanhùa. Okay. First step — **nǐ qù yóujú.**
telephone call   go   post office

(shr) *(how)*   *(dway-hwah)*
The following **shì yí ge hǎo** sample **dùihùa. Xìanzài** familiarize yourself with these **cí.**
             is   (C) good   conversation

Don't wait until your holiday.

Dùibùqǐ. Wǒ zài
nǎr mǎi yóupìao?

Zài qī hǎo
          number
guìtái.

- ☐ **qín** *(cheen)* . . . . musical instrument
- ☐ **fēngqín** *(fung-cheen)* . . . . organ
- ☐ **kǒuqín** *(koh-cheen)* . . . . harmonica
- ☐ **mùqín** *(moo-cheen)* . . . . xylophone
- ☐ **tíqín** *(tee-cheen)* . . . . violin

琴
qín

_____
_____
_____
_____

 Wǒ xūyào liǎng zhǎng yóupiào hé liǎng zhǎng míngxìnpiàn.

 Hángkōngxìn ma?

Míngxìnpiàn, qī máo (7); yóupiào, yì máo (1).

Dūoshǎo qían?

Shì, hángkōngxìn. Wǒ xiǎng yào liǎng zhǎng Zhōngguó míngxìnpiàn. Dūoshǎo qían?

Yì máo (1).

Hǎo!

Zhèr shì míngxìnpiàn hé yóupiào.

Xìexie.

Next step — **nǐ** ask **wèntí** like those **xìabianrde,** *(ssee-ah-bee-ahnr-duh)* depending upon what **nǐ** want.
below

(zi) *(nahr)* *(my)* *(yoh-pee-ow)*
Wǒ zài nǎr mǎi yóupìao?
am where buy stamps

(my) *(meeng-sseen-pee-ahn)*
Wǒ zài nǎr mǎi míngxìnpìan?
buy postcards

(yoh) *(goong-goong)* *(dee-ahn-hwah)*
Nǎr yǒu gōnggòng dìanhùa?
is public telephone

(nahr)(dah) *(chahng-too)* *(dee-ahn-hwah)*
Wǒ zài nar dǎ chángtú dìanhùa?
where make long-distance telephone call

(dah) *(buhn-dee)*
Wǒ zài nǎr dǎ běndì dìanhùa?
make local telephone call

(dah) *(dee-ahn-bow)*
Wǒ zài nǎr dǎ dìanbào?
make telegram

(jee) *(bow-gwo)*
Wǒ zài nǎr jì bāogǔo?
send parcel

(dah)
Wǒ zài nǎr dǎ dìanhùa?
make telephone call

(dwo-show) *(chee-ahn)*
Dūoshǎo qían?
how much money

(yoh) *(yoh-twong)*
Nǎr yǒu yóutǒng?
is mailbox

Practice these sentences again and again.

Xìanzài, quiz yourself. See if **nǐ** can translate the following thoughts into **Zhōngwén.**

The answers are at the bottom of the **xìa** **yè.** *(ssee-ah)* *(yeh)*
next page

1. Where is a telephone booth? *Dìanhùa tíng zài nǎr?*

2. Where do I make a phone call? _____

3. Where do I make a local phone call? _____

4. Where do I make a long-distance phone call? _____

5. Where is the post office? _____

□ **máo** *(mow)* . . . . wool
□ **máobǐ** *(mow-bee)* . . . . writing brush
□ **máojīn** *(mow-jeen)* . . . . towel
□ **máopí** *(mow-pee)* . . . . fur
□ **máoyī** *(mow-yee)* . . . . sweater

毛
mao

62

6. Where do I buy stamps?_____

7. Airmail stamps? _____

8. Where do I send a package? _____

9. Where do I send/make a telegram? _____

hào
10. Where is counter (number) eight? _____

(juhr) (yoh) (jee) (guh) (dwong-tsr)
Zhèr yǒu jǐ ge dòngcí.
here are several (C) verbs

(dah)
dǎ = to make (telephone   *(ssee-eh)* **xiě** = to write   *(gay)* **gěi** = to give   *(gay) (chee-ahn)* **gěi qian** = to give/
call, telegram)   pay money

_____*dǎ*_____   _____

(dah)
dǎ
make

Wǒ _____ **yí ge dìanhùa.** *(dee-ahn-hwah)*
one (C) telephone call

Nǐ _____ **yí ge dìanbào.** *(dee-ahn-bow)*
telegram

Tā bù *(boo)* _____*dǎ*_____ **dianhùa.** *(dee-ahn-hwah)*
not

Wǒmen _____ **hěn dūo dìanhùa.** *(huhn) (dwo)*
very many

Tāmen bù *(boo)* _____ **dianbào.** *(dee-ahn-bow)*
not   telegram

(gay)
gěi
give

Wǒ _____ **tā yì běn shū.** *(tah) (buhn) (shoo)*
him (C) book

Nǐ _____*gěi*_____ **wǒ sì zhāng míngxìnpìan.** *(wo) (sr)(jahng) (meeng-sseen-pee-ahn)*
me four postcards

Tā _____ **tāmen hěn dūo qían.** *(tah-muhn) (huhn) (dwo) (chee-ahn)*
them very much money

Wǒmen _____ **tā bā zhāng yóupìao.** *(tah) (bah) (yoh-pee-ow)*
her eight (C) stamps

Tāmen _____ **nǐ shénme?** *(nee)*
you what

(ssee-eh)
xiě
write

Wǒ _____ **yì fēng xìn.** *(fuhng) (sseen)*
(C) letter

Nǐ _____*xiě*_____ **wǔ ge zì.** *(woo)*
five (C)

Tā _____ **hěn dūo zì.** *(huhn) (dwo)*
very many

Wǒmen _____ **shénme?**
what

Tāmen bù *(boo)* _____ **shénme?**
not

(gay) (chee-ahn)
gěi qian
give/pay money

Wǒ _____*gěi*_____ **yì běn shūde** *(buhn) (shoo-duh)* _____*qían*_____.
(C) book's

Nǐ _____ **qìanbǐde** *(chee-ahng-bee-duh)* _____.
pencil's

Tā _____ **gāngbǐde** *(gahng-bee-duh)* _____.
pen's

Wǒmen _____ **wǔ zhāng yóupìaode** *(jahng) (yoh-pee-ow-duh)* ___.
(C) stamp's

Tāmen _____ **shénmede** _____?
for what

63

Step 16

(shoh-jyew)   *(jahng-dahn)*
Shǒujù hùoshì Zhàngdān
receipt   or   bill

(zi) *(yow)* *(gay)* *(chee-ahn)* *(jahng-dahn)*
Zài Zhōngguó, nǐ yào gěi qian for zhàngdán. **Nǐ** have just finished your evening meal and **nǐ**
in   will give/pay money   bills

(ssee-ahng) *(yow)* *(gay)* *(chee-ahn)*   *(gay)*   *(jee-ow)* *(foo-woo-yew-ahn)*   *(twong-jr)*
xiǎng yào gěi qián. **Nǐ zěnme gěi qián?** **Nǐ jiao** the **fúwùyúan:**   **"Tóngzhì?"**
would like give/pay money   how   pay   call   service person   comrade

Dùibùqǐ. Qǐng gěi wǒ zhàngdānr.

Hǎo.

(foo-woo-yew-ahn)
The **fúwùyúan** will normally reel off what **nǐ**
service person

have eaten, while writing rapidly. Then the

(foo-woo-yew-ahn) *(gay)*   *(dahn-zr)* *(jr)*
fúwùyúan will **gěi** you **yì zhāng dānzi** of **zhǐ**
give (C)   slip   paper

that looks like the **zhàngdán** in the **hùar,**
bill

while saying something like

(yee-goong) *(lee-oh)* *(yew-ahn)* *(mow)*
"Yígòng lìu   yúan lìu máo."
altogether six

(jahng-dahn)   *(hwo-shr)* *(gay)*
Then, you will take your **zhàngdán** to the counter to pay the cashier **hùoshì nǐ gěi**
bill   or   give

(chee-ahn)
fúwùyúan qían and **zhàngdán.** The **fúwùyúan** will then bring you your change.
money

Remember that, in **Zhōngguó,** it is not customary to leave a tip.

Also do not be surprised if the **fúwùyúan** does not thank you — this is also not a custom in

Zhōngguó.

Qían zài zhèr.

Xièxie.

(sseen)
Sound confusing? No, just **xīn** and different.
new

☐ **dòu** *(doh)*	bean		_____
☐ **dòufu** *(doh-foo)*	bean curd		_____
☐ **dòushā** *(doh-shah)*	bean paste	豆	_____
☐ **dòuyá** *(doh-yah)*	bean sprout	*dou*	_____
☐ **dòuyóu** *(doh-yoh)*	soybean oil		_____

Also, remember to reserve a table in advance if you are planning to dine out in **Zhōngguó**. Give yourself enough time to enjoy a cup of **chá** and to read the *(tsi-dahn)* **càidān** thoroughly before you order. If you find toward the end of your meal that you cannot finish, the *(foo-woo-yew-ahn)* **fúwùyuán** will wrap up your meal for you to take with you.

To familiarize yourself with the dining customs in **Zhōngguó,** watch the other *(ruhn)* **rén** in the **fànguǎnr.** At first, it seems foreign (which it is!) but **nǐ** will catch on quickly and your familiarity with **Zhōngguó** customs will be appreciated. *(juhr)* **Zhèr** *(shr)* **shì yí ge** sample *(dway-hwah)* **duìhuà** that involves paying the *(jahng-dahn)* **zhàngdān** when leaving a **lǚguǎn.**

Zhāng sān: *(dway-boo-chee)* **Duìbùqǐ.** **Wǒ xiǎng yào qīng zhàng.**
excuse me · would like · clear · account

Lǚguǎn jīnglǐ: *(jeeng-lee)* *(cheeng-wuhn)* **Qǐngwèn nǎ ge fángjiān?**
hotel · manager · may I ask · which (C) · room

Zhāng sān: **Sān bǎi yīshí hào.**
hundred · number

Lǚguǎn jīnglǐ: *(ssee-eh-ssee-eh)* **Xièxie.** *(cheeng)* **Qǐng** *(dung)* **děng** *(yee)* **yí** *(ssee-ah)* **xia.**
thank you · please · wait · a · little

Lǚguǎn jīnglǐ: **Zhèr shì nǐde** *(nee-duh)* **zhàngdān.** *(yee-goong)* **Yígòng sān bǎi èrshíwǔ yúan.**
your · bill · altogether · hundred

Zhāng sān: *(ssee-eh-ssee-eh)* **Xièxie.** (**Zhāng sān** hands him **sān bǎi sānshí yúan.**)
thank you

Lǚguǎn jīnglǐ: **Zhèr shì nǐde** *(nee-duh)(shoh-jyew)(huh)* **shǒujù hé wǔ yúan.** *(ssee-eh-ssee-eh)* **Xièxie.**
you · receipt · and

Simple, right? If **nǐ** *(yoh)* **yǒu** *(ruhn-huh)* **rènhé** *(wuhn-tee)* **wèntí** with *(shoo-zr)* **shùzì,** just ask someone to write out the
have · any · questions · numbers

shùzì so that **nǐ** can be sure you understand everything correctly.

(cheeng)(ssee-eh)(choo)(juh) **Qǐng xiě chǔ zhè shùzì.** *(ssee-eh-ssee-eh)* **Xièxie.**
please · write · out · this

Let's take a break from **qián** *(chee-ahn)* and, starting on the next **yè** *(yeh)*, learn some **xīn cí.** *(sseen)*
money · page · new

☐ **mì** *(mee)* . . . . honey
☐ **mìfēng** *(mee-fung)* . . . . honeybee
☐ **mìjiàn** *(mee-jee-ahn)* . . . . candied fruit
☐ **mìjú** *(mee-jyew)* . . . . tangerine
☐ **mìyuè** *(mee-yew-eh)* . . . . honeymoon

蜜
mi

(jee-ahn-kahng)
Tā jiànkāng.
healthy

(beeng) (luh)
Tā bìng le.
sick

(nah) (how)
Nà hǎo.
that good

(nah) (boo) (how)
Nà bù hǎo.
that not good

(nah) (hwy)
Nà huài.
that bad

(shway) (shr) (wuhn)(duh)
Shuǐ shì wēn de.
water is warm

(woo-shr) (doo)
Shuǐ shì wǔshí dù.
fifty degrees

(lung)
Shuǐ shì lěng dé.
cold

(jr) (yoh) (shr-chee) (doo)
Zhǐ yǒu shíqī dù.
only have seventeen degrees

 xǐao

DÀ

(ssee-ow) (shung) (shwo-hwah)
Tā xǐao shēng shūohùa.
small voice speak

(dah) (shung) (shwo-hwah)
Tā dà shēng shūohùa.
big voice speak

(hohng) (ssee-ahn)(dwahn)
Hóng xìan dǔan.
red line short

(lahn) (ssee-ahn) (chahng)
Lán xìan chǎng.
blue line long

(juh) (guh) (new-ruhn) (gow)
Zhè ge nürén gāo.
this (C) woman tall

(ssee-ow-hir) (i)
Zhè ge xǐaoháir ǎi.
child short

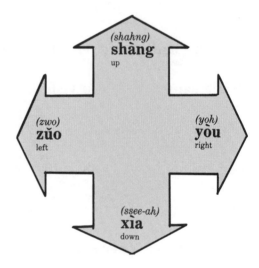

(shahng)
shàng
up

(zwo)
zǔo
left

(yoh)
yòu
right

(ssee-ah)
xìa
down

(juh) (buhn) (hohng) (hoh)
Zhè běn hóng shū hòu.
this (C) red thick

(lew) (bow)
Zhè běn lǜ shū báo.
(C) green thin

(goong-lee)(yee) (jung-toh)
20 gōnglǐ/yì zhōngtóu
kilometers one hour

(mahn)
màn
slow

(goong-lee)(yee) (jung-toh)
750 gōnglǐ/yì zhōngtóu
kilometers one hour

(kwy)
kùai
fast

☐ **níu** *(nee-oh)* . . . . cow
☐ **níudú** *(nee-oh-doo)* . . . . calf
☐ **níujǐao** *(nee-oh-jee-ow)* . . . . horn
☐ **níuláng** *(nee-oh-lahng)* . . . . cowherd
☐ **níunǎi** *(nee-oh-ni)* . . . . cow's milk

牛
niu

(juh) (zwo) (shahn) (gow)   *(lee-ahng) (chee-ahn) (goong-chr) (gow)*
Zhè zùo shān gāo. Liǎng qiān gōngchǐ gāo.
this (C) mountain tall   two thousand meters tall

(zwo) (shahn) (dee)   *(jr) (yoh) (goong-chr) (gow)*
Zhè zùo shān dī. Zhǐ yǒu 800 gōngchǐ gāo.
(C) mountain low only have meters tall

(zoo-foo) (low)   *(sway)*
Zǔfù lǎo: tā 70 sùi.
grandfather old age (C)

(ssee-ow-hir) (nee-ahn-cheeng)   *(tsi) (sway)*
Xǐaoháir níanqīng. Tā cái 10 sùi.
child young only age (C)

(huhn) (gway) (yee) (tee-ahn) (yow)
Lǚguǎn hěn gùi. Yì tīan yào 60 yúan.
very expensive one day costs

(goong-yew) (pee-ahn-yee) (tee-ahn) (yow)
Gōngyù píanyi. Yì tīan yào 20 yúan.
boarding room inexpensive day costs

(yoh)   *(yoh-chee-ahn) (nah) (shr) (huhn) (dwo) (chee-ahn)*
Wǒ yǒu 1,000 yúan. Wǒ yǒuqían. Nà shì hěn dūo qían.
have   rich that is very much money

(yoh)   *(chee-wong)*   *(show-duh) (chee-ahn)*
Tā zhǐ yǒu 10 yúan. Tā qíong. Nà shì hěn shǎode qían.
only has poor little money

(juhr) (yoh) (sr)(guh) (sseen) (dwong-tsr)
Zhèr yǒu sì ge xīn dòngcí.
here are four (C) new

(jr-dow)
zhǐdào = to know

(nung)
néng = to be able to/can

(yeeng-gi)
yīnggāi = to have to/ should

(kahn)
kàn = to read

zhīdào _____ _____ _____

(jr-dow) (nung) (yeeng-gi) (kahn) (sr)
Zhǐdào, néng, yīnggāi and **kàn** are **sì ge** important and useful verbs. Whether you are
know be able to should read

speaking about **wǒ, nǐ, tā, wǒmen, nǐmen** or **tāmen**, remember that verbs remain the same

in the **Zhōngguó hùa**.

☐ **níupái** *(nee-oh-pi)* . . . . beefsteak
☐ **níupí** *(nee-oh-pee)* . . . . leather
☐ **níupízhǐ** *(nee-oh-pee-jr)* . . . . brown paper
☐ **níuròu** *(nee-oh-roh)* . . . . beef
☐ **níuwěi** *(nee-oh-way)* . . . . ox tail

牛
niu

_____
_____
_____
_____
_____

67

Study the following **dòngcí** closely as you will use them a lot.

(nung)
néng
be able to/can

Wǒ _____ kàn Zhōngwén.
(kahn) read

Nǐ _néng_ shūo Zhōngwén.
(shwo) speak

Tā _____ dǒng Zhōngwén.
(dwong) understand

Wǒmen _____ dǒng Yīngwén.

Tāmen _____ kàn Zhōngwén.
read

(yeeng-gi)
yīnggāi
have to/should

Wǒ _____ shūo Zhōngwén.
(shwo) speak

Nǐ _____ kàn shū.
(kahn) read

Tā _yīnggāi_ shūo Yīngwén.

Wǒmen _____ dǒng Zhōngwén.
(dwong) understand

Tāmen _____ kàn bàozhǐ.
(kahn) (bow-jr) read newspaper

(jr-dow)
zhīdào
know

Wǒ _zhīdào_ nà ge.
(nah) (guh) that (C)

Nǐ _____ yìdiǎnr Zhōngwén.
(yee-dee-ahnr) a little

Tā _____ hěn dūo.
(huhn) (dwo) very much

Wǒmen _____ hěn shǎo.
(show) little

Tāmen bù _____ .

(kahn)
kàn
read

Wǒ _____ shū.

Nǐ _____ zázhì.
(zah-jr) magazine

Tā _____ míngxìnpiàn.
(meeng-sseen-pee-ahn) postcard

Wǒmen _kàn_ biǎogé.
(bee-ow-guh) form

Tāmen _____ hěn dūo.
(huhn) (dwo) very much

(nung)
Nǐ néng translate these thoughts into **Zhōngwén ma?** The answers **zài xiàbīanr.**
can

1. I can speak Chinese. _____

2. He should pay now. _____

3. We do not know. _____

4. They can pay. _____

5. She knows very little. _____

6. I can speak a little Chinese. _____

Xìanzài draw **xìan** *(ssee-ahn)* between the **xìabìanrde** *(ssee-ah-bee-ahnr-duh)* opposites. Don't forget to say them out loud.
lines *below*

Use these **cí** every day to describe **dōngxi zài** *(dwong-ssee)* **nǐde** *(nee-duh)* **fángzi,** **nǐde** *(nee-duh)* **xúexìao,** *(ssee-yew-eh-ssee-ow)* **nǐde** *(nee-duh)*
things *your* *your* *school* *your*

bàngōngshì, *(bahn-goong-shr)* etc.
office

(dah) **dà** ———————————— *(shahng)* **shàng**

(ssee-ah) **xìa** *(dee)* **dǐ**

(nee-ahn-cheeng) **nìanqīng** *(ssee-ow)* **xìao**

(chee-wong) **qíong** *(dah)(shung)* **dà shēng**

(jee-ahn-kahng) **jìankāng** *(bow)* **báo**

(chahng) **cháng** *(pee-ahn-yee)* **píanyi**

(dwo) **dūo** *(show)* **shǎo**

(how) **hǎo** *(beeng)* **bìng**

(hoh) **hòu** *(low)* **lǎo**

(gow) **gāo** *(kwy)* **kùai**

(wuhn) **wēn** *(yoh)* **yòu**

(zwo) **zǔo** *(lung)* **lěng**

(mahn) **màn** *(yoh-chee-ahn)* **yǒuqían**

(gway) **gùi** *(hwy)* **hùai**

(ssee-ow) *(shung)* **xìao shēng** *(dwahn)* **dǔan**

☐ **yǐ** *(yee)* .... chair
☐ **chángyǐ** *(chahng-yee)* .... bench
☐ **tǎngyǐ** *(tahng-yee)* .... recliner
☐ **yáoyǐ** *(yow-yee)* .... rocking chair
☐ **zhùanyǐ** *(jwahn-yee)* .... swivel chair

椅
yi

_____
_____
_____
_____
_____

69

Step 17

(lew-sseeng)
Lǚxíng, Lǚxíng, Lǚxíng
travel

(zwo-tee-ahn) (dow)
Zúotian dào Nánjīng!
yesterday   to

(jeen-tee-ahn)
Jīntian dào Shànghǎi!
today

(meeng-tee-ahn)
Míngtian dào Běijīng!
tomorrow

(sseeng-chee-yee) (zi)
Xīngqīyī zài Gǔangzhōu!
Monday   in

(sseeng-chee-sahn)
Xīngqīsān zài Hànkǒu!
Wednesday

(sseeng-chee-woo)
Xīngqīwǔ zài Xīān!
Friday

(lew-sseng)(huhn) (rohng-yee)   *(ruhn) (doh)*
Zài Zhōnggúo, lǚxíng hěn róngyì. Zhōnggúo rén dōu hěn helpful. **Zhōnggúo**
travel   very   easy   people   all

(huh)   *(chah-boo-dwo) (yee-yahng) (dah)*   *(yoh) (huhn) (dwo) (fahng-fah)*
hé Měigúo chàbùdūo yíyàng dà. Zài Zhōnggúo, yǒu hěn dūo fāngfǎ lǚxíng:
and   about   same   size   very   many   ways

(zwo) (hwo-chuh)
zùo hǔoche
by/sit train

(goong-goong-chee-chuh))
zùo gōnggòngqìchē
bus

(sahn-loon-chuh)
zùo sānlunchě
pedicab

(hwo-shr)   *(fay-jee)*
hùoshì zùo fēijī
or   airplane

(chwahn)
hùoshì zùo chúan
boat

(chee) (zr-sseeng-chuh)
hùoshì qí zìxíngchē.
astride bicycle

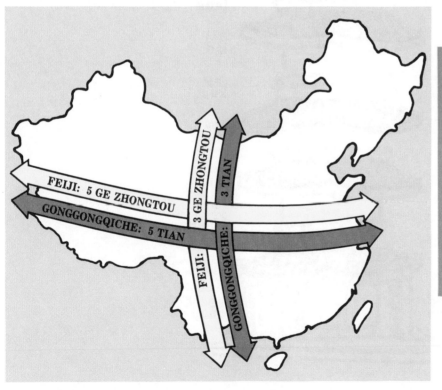

FEIJI: 5 GE ZHONGTOU

GONGGONGQICHE: 5 TIAN

3 GE ZHONGTOU

FEIJI:

GONGGONGQICHE:

3 TIAN

(zwo-bee-ahnr)
Zǔobīanr shì Zhōnggúo
left

(dee-too) (tswong) (dwong) (dow)
dìtú. Cóng dōng dào
map   from   east   to

(fay-jee)
xī, lǚxíng zùo fēijī
airplane

(jung-toh)
wǔ ge zhōngtóu;
hours

(goong-goong-chee-chuh)
zùo gōnggòngqìchē
bus

(tee-ahn)
wǔ tian.
days

☐ **gǔan** *(gwahn)* . . . . place, hall
☐ **bówùgǔan** *(bwo-woo-gwahn)* . . . . museum
☐ **chágǔan** *(chah-gwahn)* . . . . teahouse
☐ **lǚgǔan** *(lew-gwahn)* . . . . hotel
☐ **lǐfàgǔan** *(lee-fah-gwahn)* . . . . barbershop

館
guan

70

Zhōngguó rén bù cháng lǚxíng *(ruhn) (boo) (chahng) (lew-sseeng)* themselves. However, because of the many **wàiguó** *(wi-gwo)*

people not often travel · foreign

visitors in **Zhōngguó, nǐ** will see many "travel" **cí.** Practice saying the following **cí** many

times. **Nǐ** will see them often.

(lew-kuh)
lǚkè
passenger, traveler

(sseeng-lee)
xínglǐ
luggage

(ssee-ahng-zr)
xiāngzi
trunk

(show-pee-ow) (choo)
shòupìao chù
ticket · office

(lew-sseeng) (shuh)
lǚxíng shè
travel · agent

Xiàbianr shì some basic signs that **nǐ yě** should learn to recognize quickly. **Wàng** means *(yeh) (wahng)*

also

"toward" or "to" in **Zhōngguó hùa.** For example "**wàng chūkǒu**" means "to the exit." *(wahng) (choo-koh)*

exit

(roo-koh)
rùkǒu _____
entrance

(jeen-jr) (twong-sseeng)
jìnzhǐ tōngxíng _____
no trespassing

(choo-koh)
chūkǒu *chūkǒu*
exit

(ti-peeng) (muhn)
tàipíng mén _____
emergency · gate

RUKOU

CHUKOU

TAIPING MEN

☐ **měishùguǎn** *(may-shoo-gwahn)* . . . . art gallery
☐ **shuǐzúguǎn** *(shway-zoo-gwahn)* . . . . aquarium
☐ **tǐyùguǎn** *(tee-yew-gwahn)* . . . . gymnasium
☐ **túshūguǎn** *(too-shoo-gwahn)* . . . . library
☐ **zhǎnlǎnguǎn** *(jahn-lahn-gwahn)* . . . . . . exhibition hall

馆
guan

_____
_____
_____
_____
_____

Familiarize yourself with the following **cí**. They will help you in your **lǔxíng** *(lew-sseeng)* travel in **Zhōngguó.**

(jee-eh)
jīe _____
street

(pee-ow)
pìao _____
ticket

(ruhn-sseeng-dow)
rénxíngdào _____
sidewalk

(dah-dow)
dàdào _____ *dàdào*
boulevard

Zhèr shì sì ge zhòngyàode cí. *(sr)* *(gwong-yow-duh)*
four (C)   important

Cóng Shànghǎi dào Nánjīng *(tswong)* *(dow)*			
from		to	
Kāi *(ki)*	**Hǔochē lèi** *(lay)*	**Dào** *(dow)*	**Fùjì** *(foo-jee)*
leave	train type	arrive	remarks
7:40	**Tèkùai**	8:30	🐎 ✗ 🚌 ☎
10:00	**Kùaichē**	11:10	✗
12:15	**Kùaichē**	13:25	✗ 🚌
14:32	**Pǔtōngchē**	16:15	

(dow)
dào _____
to arrive

(ki)
kāi _____
to leave, to depart

(gwo-jee)
gúojì _____
international

(gwo-nay)
gúonèi _____
domestic

Let's learn the basic travel **dòngcí**. *(dwong-tsr)* Follow the same pattern **nǐ** learned **yǐqían**. *(yee-chee-ahn)* Remember that verbs do not have different endings.

(ki-chuh)
kāichē = to drive

(fay)
fēi = to fly

(dah)
dā = to take (means of transportation)

_____

(deeng)
dìng = to reserve

(jee-ahng-lwo)
jìanglùo = to land

(dow)
dào = to arrive

_____

(ki)
kāi = to leave, to depart

(shahng)
shàng = to climb/ to get on

(hwahn) (chuh)
hùan (chē) = to transfer (vehicle)

_____

(zwo)
zùo = to sit

(shahng) (chuh)
shàng (chē) = to board (vehicle)
on

(ssee-ah) (chuh)
xìa (chē) = to disembark (vehicle)
down

zùo

- ☐ **mǐ** *(mee)* .... rice
- ☐ **mǐfàn** *(mee-fahn)* .... cooked rice
- ☐ **mǐfěn** *(mee-fuhn)* .... rice noodle
- ☐ **mǐjǐu** *(mee-jee-oh)* .... rice wine
- ☐ **mǐsè** *(mee-suh)* .... cream-colored

米
mi

_____

72

With **zhè xiē dòngcí, nǐ** are ready for any *(lew-sseeng)* **lǚxíng** anywhere. Using the **dòngcí** that
travel
(yee-chee-ahn) (lee-ahn-ssee-duh)
nǐ yǐqían **lìanxíde,** translate the following sentences and questions into **Zhōngwén.** The
before   practiced
(ssee-ah-bee-ahnr)
answers **zài xìabìanr.**

1. I fly to Nanjing._____

2. I drive to Shanghai._____

3. We land in Peking._____

4. He sits in the airplane._____

5. She books the trips to America._____

6. They travel to Hangzhou._____

7. Where is the train to Xian?_____

8. How do I fly to Japan?_____

(juhr) (yoh) *(sseen)*
Zhèr yòu are more **xīn cí** for your trip. As always, write out the **cí** and practice the sample
here   again   new

sentences out loud.

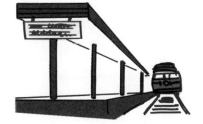

(hwo-chuh) (jahn)
hǔochē zhàn
train   station

(hwo-chuh) (zwong-jahn)
hǔochē zǒngzhàn
train   main station

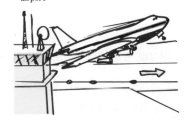

(fay-jee-chahng)
fēijīchǎng
airport

fēijīchǎng

_____

(dway-boo-chee) (hwo-chuh) (jahn)
Dùibùqǐ. Hǔochē zhàn
excuse me   train   station
(zi) (nahr)
zài nǎr?
is   where

_____

Dùibùqǐ. Hǔochē
train
(zwong-jahn)
zǒngzhàn zài nǎr?
main station

(fay-jee-chahng)
Dùibùqǐ. Fēijīchǎng zài nǎr?
airport

(dway-hwahn) (choo)
dùihùan chù
money-exchange office

DÙIHÙAN CHÙ

YUAN YEN DM
£ $

(shr-woo-jow-leeng)
shīwùzhāolíng
lost-and-found office

SHĪWÙZHĀOLÍNG

(shr-jee-ahn) (bee-ow)
shíjian biao
time   schedule

(tswong) Cóng Shànghǎi dào Nánjīng *(dow)*			
(ksi) **Kāi** leave	**Hùochē lèi** train type *(lay)*	*(dow)* **Dào** arrive	*(foo-jee)* **Fùjì** remarks
7:40	Tèkùai	8:30	
10:00	Kùaichē	11:10	
12:15	Kùaichē	13:25	
14:32	Pùtōngchē	16:15	

(dway-boo-chee) (dway-hwahn) (choo)
Dùibùqǐ. Dùihùan chù
excuse me
(zi) (nahr)
zài nǎr?
is where

(shr-woo-jow-leeng)
Dùibùqǐ. Shīwùzhāolíng
lost-and-found office

zài nǎr?

(shr-jee-ahn) (bee-ow)
Dùibùqǐ. Shíjian biao
time schedule

zài nǎr?

(yoh-ruhn)
yǒurén _____ *yǒurén*
occupied

(chuh-ssee-ahng)
chēxiang _____
compartment

(zwo-way)
zùowèi _____
seat

(juh) (guh) (zwo-way) (yoh-ruhn) (mah)
Zhè ge   zùowèi yǒurén ma? _____
this   (C)   seat   occupied

(chuh-ssee-ahng) (yoh-ruhn) (mah)
Zhè ge chēxiang   yǒurén ma? _____
this   (C)   compartment   occupied

Practice writing out the following **wèntí**. It will help you *(yee-hoh)* **yǐhòu.**
later

(cheeng-wuhn) (tsuh-swo)
Qǐngwèn, cèsǔo zài nǎr? _____
may I ask   lavatory
(jee-oh) (how) (chuh-ssee-ahng)
Jǐu   hào chēxiang zài nǎr?
nine   number compartment
(hoh-chuh) (shr)
Hòuchē shì zài nǎr? ___ *Hòuchē shì zài nǎr?*
waiting   room
(bah) (how) (gway-ti)
Bá hào gùitái zài nǎr? _____
eight   number counter
(kuh-yee) (choh-yahn) (mah)
Kěyǐ   chōuyān ma? _____
may (I)   smoke

☐ **yùe** *(yew-eh)* .... month, moon
☐ **yùebào** *(yew-eh-bow)* .... monthly magazine
☐ **yùeliang** *(yew-eh-lee-ahng)* .... moon
☐ **yùesè** *(yew-eh-suh)* .... moonlight
☐ **yùe yè** *(yew-eh) (yeh)* .... moonlit night

月
yue
_____
_____
_____

74

Increase your travel **cí** by writing out the **xìabīanrde cí** *(ssee-ah-bee-ahnr-duh)* and practicing the sample sentences out loud.
below

(dow)
dào _____
to
　　　Dào Shànghǎi de huǒchē zài nǎr?

(shr-jee-ahn)
shíjiān _____
time
　　　Wǒ yǒu hěn dūo shíjiān.

(tee-eh-gway)
tiěguǐ _____
track
　　　Huǒchē cóng dìqī tíao tiěguǐ kāi.
　　　　　　seventh (C)

(yew-eh-ti)
yuètái _____
platform
　　　Huǒchē dào dìbā yuètái.
　　　　　　eighth

Practice these **cí** every day. **Nǐ** will be surprised how often **nǐ** will use them.

(ssee-ah-bee-ahnr-duh)(nung) (kahn-dung)
Xìabīanrde nǐ néng kàndǒng ma?
　　　　　　　　can　　read

Xìanzài nǐ zùo zài fēi wǎng Zhōnggúo de fēijī shàng. *(zwo)(fay)(wahng)(fay-jee)(shahng)* **Nǐ yǒu le pìao hé hùzhào.** *(yoh)(pee-ow)(huh)(hoo-jow)*
　　　　　sit　　fly　to　　　　　　　airplane　on　　have　ticket　and　passport
Nǐ dài le nǐde xīangzi. *(di)(nee-duh)(ssee-ahng-zr)* **Xìanzài nǐ shì yí ge lǚkè.** *(shr)(lew-kuh)* **Nǐ shísì dǐan shíwǔ fēn zài** *(shr-sr)(dee-ahn)(shr-woo)(fuhn)*
bring　your　suitcase　　　　are　(C)　traveler　fourteen o'clock　fifteen　minutes
Zhōnggúo jìanglùo. *(jee-ahng-lwo)* **Yílùpíngān!** *(yee-loo-peeng-ahn)*
land　　　　　　　safe and peaceful journey

Xìanzài nǐ dàole *(dow-luh)* and you **qù** *(chee-yew)* to the **huǒchē zhàn** *(jahn)* in order to get to your final destination.
have arrived　　　　　go　　　　train　station

Zhōnggúo huǒchē come in different shapes, sizes and speeds. **Zài Zhōnggúo,** there are

pǔtōngchē, kùaichē hé tèbíe kùaichē. *(poo-twong-chuh)(kwy-chuh)(tuh-bee-uh)(kwy-chuh)* Some **huǒchē yǒu cānchē.** *(yoh)(tsahn-chuh)* Some **huǒchē yǒu**
ordinary trains　fast trains　special　fast trains　　　　　　　　　　has　dining car
wòpù. *(wo-poo)* Some **huǒchē yǒu tǎngyǐ.** *(yoh)(tahng-yee)* All this will be indicated on the **shíjiān bǐao,** *(shr-jee-ahn)(bee-ow)* but
sleeping car　　　　　　　　reclining car　　　　　　　　　　　　　　　　　　time　schedule
remember, **nǐ** should **zhīdào zěnme wèn zhè xīe wèntí.** *(jr-dow)(wuhn)(juh)(wuhn-tee)* Practice your possible **wèntí**
　　　　　know　how　to ask　these　questions

by writing out the following examples.

(juh) (guh) (hwo-chuh)(yoh) (tsahn-chuh)
Zhè ge huǒchē yǒu cānchē ma? _____
this　(C)　train　has　dining car
(wo-poo)
Zhè ge huǒchē yǒu wòpù ma? _____
　(C)　　　　　sleeping car
(tahng-yee)
Zhè ge huǒchē yǒu tǎngyǐ ma? _____
　(C)　　　　　reclining car

☐ **èryùe** *(ur-yew-eh)* .... February
☐ **jǐuyùe** *(jee-oh-yew-eh)* .... September
☐ **lìuyùe** *(lee-oh-yew-eh)* .... June
☐ **shíyīyùe** *(shr-yee-yew-eh)* .... November
☐ **sìyùe** *(sr-yew-eh)* .... April

月
yue

_____
_____
_____
_____
_____

75

What about inquiring about **jiaqian?** *(jee-ah-chee-ahn)* prices **Nǐ néng** *(nung)* can **wèn** *(wuhn)* ask **zhè ge wèntí.** (C)

Cóng Shànghǎi dào Běijīng dūoshǎo qián? *(tswong)* from *(dow)* to *(dwo-show)* how much *(chee-ahn)* money _____

dānchéng *(dahn-chung)* one-way _____ **láihúi** *(li-hway)* round-trip *láihúi*

Cóng Shànghǎi dào Nánjīng dūoshǎo qián? *(tswong)* from *(dow)* to _____

Dānchéng háishì láihúi? *(dahn-chung)* one-way *(hi-shr)* or *(li-hway)* round-trip _____

Nǐ yě néng wèn: *(yeh)* also *(nung)* can *(wuhn)* ask

Shénme shíhòu kāi? *(shr-hoh)* *(ki)* what time depart

Shénme shíhòu dào? *(dow)* arrive

Hǔochē shénme shíhòu kāi Gǔangzhōu? *(hwo-chuh)* train *(ki)* depart _____

Fēijī shénme shíhòu kāi Shànghǎi? *(fay-jee)* airplane _____

Hǔochē shénme shíhòu dào Xīān? *(dow)* arrive _____

Fēijī shénme shíhòu dào Běijīng? *(dow)* arrive _____

Nǐ dàole Zhōnggúo. have arrived **Xīanzài nǐ zài hǔochē zhàn.** are at *(jahn)* station **Nǐ yào qù nǎr?** *(yow)* want *(chee-yew)* to go *(nahr)* where **Hǎo, tell that to** *(how)* well the **màipìaodè** *(my-pee-ow-duh)* ticket seller at the **gùitái.** *(gway-ti)* counter

Wǒ xǐang yào dào Hángzhōu qù. *(ssee-ahng)* would *(yow)* like *(dow)* to *(chee-yew)* go _____

Wǒ xǐang yào dào Sūzhōu qù. *(dow)* to *(chee-yew)* go *Wǒ xǐang yào dào Sūzhōu qù.*

Wǒmen xǐang yào dào Běidàihé qù. _____

Dào Tīanjīn de chē shénme shíhòu kāi? *(dow)* to *(chuh)* train what *(shr-hoh)* time *(ki)* leave _____

Dào Tīanjīn de pìao dūoshǎo qían? *(pee-ow)* ticket *(dwo-show)* how much *(chee-ahn)* money _____

Wǒ xǐang yào yì zhāng pìao. *(yee)* one *(jahng)* (C) *(pee-ow)* ticket _____

Tóu děng *(toh)* *(dung)* first class _____ **Èr děng** *(ur)* *(dung)* second class _____

Shì dānchéng háishì láihúi? *(shr)* is *(dahn-chung)* one-way *(hi-shr)* or *(li-hway)* round-trip _____

Yào hùanchē ma? *(yow)* *(hwahn-chuh)* have to transfer _____ **Xìexie.** *(ssee-eh-ssee-eh)* thank you _____

With this practice, **nǐ zài** *(zi)* are off and running. **Zhè xīe lǚxíng cí** *(juh)* these *(C)* *(lew-sseeng)* travel will make your holiday

twice as enjoyable and at least three times as easy. Review the **xīn cí** *(sseen)* new by doing the

crossword puzzle on page 77. Practice drilling yourself on this step by selecting

other locations and asking your own **wèntí** about **huǒchē, gōnggòngqìchē hùoshì fēijī**
(wuhn-tee) *(hwo-chuh)* *(goong-goong-chee-chuh)* *(hwo-shr)* *(fay-jee)*
questions — trains — buses — or — airplanes

that go there. Select **xīn cí** from your **zìdǐan** and practice asking **wèntí** that begin with
(zr-dee-ahn)

NǍR	**SHÉNME SHÍHÒU**	**DŪOSHǍO QÍAN**	**hùoshì** making statements like
(nahr)	*(shr-hoh)*	*(dwo-show) (chee-ahn)*	*(hwo-shr)* or

Wǒ xǐang yào dào Shànghǎi qù.
(dow) *(chee-yew)*
to — go

Wǒ xǐang yào yì zhāng pìao.
(jahng) (pee-ow)
(C) ticket

ACROSS

2. time schedule
5. price
6. airport
10. exit
12. main station
14. passenger
15. money-exchange office
16. emergency gate
18. to travel
20. reclining car
21. luggage
23. one-way
25. to know
26. fast

DOWN

1. counter
3. train
4. ticket seller
7. to land
8. lost-and-found office
9. entrance
11. dining car
13. compartment
17. international
19. to disembark from a vehicle
22. round-trip
24. sleeping car

6. F E I J I C H A N G

23. B A N C H E N G

Step 18

(tsi-dahn)
Càidān
menu

Xiànzài nǐ zài Zhōngguó de lǚguǎn le. Nǐ è le. Nǐ xiǎng yào chīfàn. Hǎo fànguǎnr
_{are in} _{hotel (lew-gwahn)} _{hungry (uh)} _{to eat meal (chr-fahn)} _{good (how)} _{restaurant (fahn-gwahnr)}

zài nǎr? First of all, **yǒu hěn duō chīfàn de dìfāng.** Let's learn them.
_{(yoh) (huhn) (chr-fahn) (dee-fahng)}
_{there are very many eating places}

lǚguǎn de shítáng (shr-tahng)	= a dining room in a hotel that serves a variety of **Zhōngguó** dishes as well as **Měiguó** dishes
xiǎo chīdiàn (ssee-ow) (chr-dee-ahn)	= a snack shop, usually open for breakfast, lunch and dinner
mìan guǎnr (mee-ahn) (gwahnr)	= a noodle shop that provides a variety of noodle dishes
jiǔ guǎnr (jee-oh) (gwahnr)	= a tavern that has a limited menu but some specialties
fànguǎnr	= a restaurant that serves a variety of meals, depending upon the province you are visiting

Try all of them. Experiment. **Nǐ** find a **hǎo fànguǎnr.** **Nǐ** enter and **zhǎo le yí ge**
_(how) _{good} _(jow) _{look for (C)}

zùowèi. **Nǐ kěyǐ** share a **zhuōzi** with others, which is a common and pleasant custom in
_(zwo-way) _(kuh-yee) _(jwo-zr)
_{seat may table}

Zhōngguó. If **nǐ kànjìan** a vacant **yǐzi,** just be sure to first ask
_(kahn-jee-ahn) _(yee-zr)
_{see chair}

Dùibùqǐ. Zhèr yǒu rén ma?
_{(dway-boo-chee) (juhr) (yoh) (ruhn) (mah)}
_{there has person}

If **nǐ xūyào yí zhāng càidān,** catch the attention of the **fúwùyúan** and say
_{(ssee-yew-yow) (jahng) (tsi-dahn)} _(foo-woo-yew-ahn)
_{need (C) menu} _{service person}

Dùibùqǐ. Wǒ kěyǐ yào yí zhāng càidān ma?
_{(kuh-yee) (yow) (tsi-dahn)}
_{may have (C) menu}

☐ **shí** (shr) . . . . stone, rock
☐ **shígāo** (shr-gow) . . . . gypsum
☐ **shíkùai** (shr-kwy) . . . . boulder   石
☐ **shímò** (shr-mwo) . . . . graphite   _{shi}
☐ **shíyīng** (shr-yeeng) . . . . quartz

Zài Zhōngguó, yǒu *(yoh)* **sān ge zhòngyàode** *(sahn)* *(jwong-yow-duh)* meals to enjoy every day, plus **xìawǔde** *(ssee-ah-woo-duh)* snacks **hé** *(huh)*

there are three (C) important   afternoon   and

wǎnshàngde *(wahn-shahng-duh)* snacks.

evening

---

zǎofàn *(zow-fahn)* = breakfast . . . **Zài lǚguǎn, nǐ** may eat **zǎofàn** between **lìu dǐan** *(dee-ahn)*

o'clock

and **bā dǐan.** Be sure to check the schedule before

you retire for the night

wǔfàn *(woo-fahn)* = lunch . . . . . Generally served from 11:30 to 14:30.

wǎnfàn *(wahn-fahn)* = dinner . . . . . Generally served from 18:00 to 20:30 and

sometimes later. After 21:00, only snacks will be

served.

If **nǐ** look around you in a **Zhōngguó fànguǎnr, nǐ** will see that **Zhōngguó rén** *(ruhn)* uses two basic

person

eating utensils: **kùaizi** *(kwy-zr)* and **tāngchí.** *(tahng-chr)* Because all **Zhōngguó cài** *(tsi)* are cut well, knives are

chopsticks   soup spoon   dishes

generally not used. Unlike **Měiguó** customs, bowls are brought to one's mouth when

eating. Before starting your meal, you may wish the people in your party

"Nín mànman chǐ." *(neen) (mahn-mahn) (chr)*

good   appetite

Xìanzài it may be **zǎofàn** *(zow-fahn)* time in Denver, but **nǐ zaì Zhōngguó** and it is **xìawǔ.** *(ssee-ah-woo)* Most

breakfast   afternoon

Zhōngguó fànguǎnr post their **càidǎn** *(tsi-dahn)* outside. Always read it before entering so **nǐ zhīdào** *(jr-dow)*

menu   will know

what type of meals and **jiaqian nǐ** *(jee-ah-chee-ahn)* will encounter inside. Most **fànguǎnr** will also write

prices

the special meal of the day on a blackboard just inside the **mén.** *(muhn)* The meal of the day is

door

always seasonal and often consists of seafood or vegetables. In addition, all the following

main categories are on the **càidǎn.** *(tsi-dahn)*

menu

□ **bǎoshí** *(bow-shr)* . . . . gem

□ **hǎi lán bǎoshí** *(hi) (lahn) (bow-shr)* . . . . . . aquamarine

□ **hóng bǎoshí** *(hohng) (bow-shr)* . . . . ruby

□ **lán bǎoshí** *(lahn) (bow-shr)* . . . . sapphire

□ **zùanshí** *(zwahn-shr)* . . . . diamond

石

shi

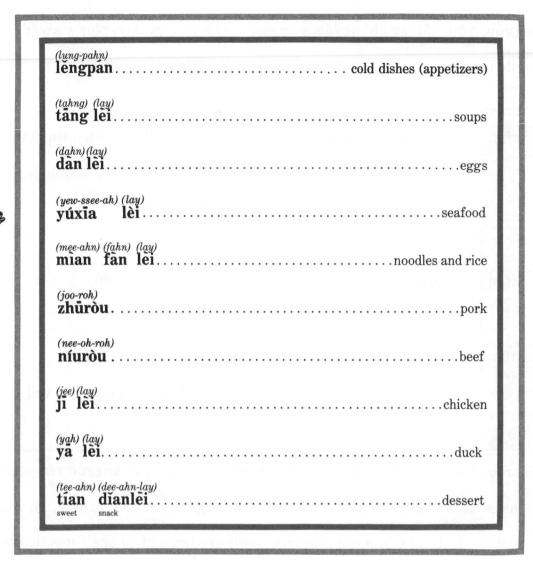

(lung-pahn)
lěngpán.. cold dishes (appetizers)

(tahng) (lay)
tāng lèi...soups

(dahn) (lay)
dàn lèi...eggs

(yew-ssee-ah) (lay)
yúxiā   lèi...seafood

(mee-ahn) (fahn) (lay)
miàn fàn lèi.............................noodles and rice

(joo-roh)
zhūròu...pork

(nee-oh-roh)
níuròu...beef

(jee) (lay)
jī lèi..chicken

(yah) (lay)
yā lèi...duck

(tee-ahn) (dee-ahn-lay)
tián diànlèi...dessert
sweet   snack

Most **fànguǎnr** also offer **náshǒucài**, *(nah-shoh-tsi)* which are the chef's special dishes. Because it is a
specialties

custom in **Zhōngguó** to share all the dishes that one's party has ordered, make sure you

know the size of the dish before you order it. The dishes will be marked in the **càidān** *(tsi-dahn)* as
menu

either large 大 , medium 中 or small 小 . At the back of this **shū,** you will find a

sample **Zhōngguó càidān.** When **nǐ** are ready to leave for **Zhōngguó,** cut out the **càidān,**

fold it and carry it in your pocket, wallet **huòshì** *(hwo-shr)* purse. **Nǐ** can **xiànzài** go into any **fànguǎnr**
or

and feel prepared!

☐ **hǎo** *(how)* .... good
☐ **hǎochī** *(how-chr)* .... delicious
☐ **hǎochù** *(how-choo)*................ benefit
☐ **hǎogǎn** *(how-gahn)* .... good impression
☐ **hǎoyì** *(how-yee)* .... goodwill

hao

In addition, learning the following should help you to identify what kind of meat **hùoshì** *(hwo-shr)* or

poultry **nǐ yào jìao** *(yow)* *(jee-ow)* and **zěnme** it will be prepared.
want to order   how

(nee-oh-roh)
níuròu

(joo-roh)
zhūròu

(yew)
yú

(jee)
jī

(yah)
yǎ

(joo)
zhǔ = boiled

(show)
shāo = roasted

(jah)
zhá = deep fried

(kow)
kǎo = baked

(jung)
zhěng = steamed

(chow)
chǎo = stir fried

Nǐ néng *(nung)* also order **qīng** *(cheeng)* **cài** *(tsi)* with your **fàn** *(fahn)*, as well as **mìan** *(mee-ahn)* or **fàn** *(fahn)*. A **tian** *(tee-ahn)* at a **càichǎng** *(tsi-chahng)*
can   fresh   vegetables   meal   noodles   rice   day   market

will teach **nǐ** the **míngzi** *(meeng-zr)* of different kinds of **cài hé shǔiguǒ** *(tsi)* *(shway-gwo)*, plus it will be a delightful
names   vegetables fruit

experience for **nǐ**. **Nǐ néng** *(nung)* always consult the menu guide at the back of this **shū** if **nǐ**
can

wàng le zhèngqùe de míngzi. *(wahng)* *(jung-chyew-eh)* **Xìanzài nǐ** have decided what **nǐ yào chī** *(chr)* and **fúwùyúan**
forget   correct   to eat

lái le. *(li)*
comes

(huh)
Hē shénme?
drink

Wǒ xǐang yào yí ge tāng *(tahng)*
soup
hé yí ge zhěng *(jung)* **yú.** *(yew)*
steamed fish

Qǐng gěi wǒ yì bēi *(cheeng)* *(gay)* *(bay)*
please give glass
píjǐu. *(pee-jee-oh)*
beer

☐ **hǎohàn** *(how-hahn)* . . . . wise man, hero _____
☐ **hǎotīng** *(how-teeng)* . . . . pleasant to the ear _____
☐ **hǎoxìao** *(how-ssee-ow)* . . . . funny _____
☐ **hǎokàn** *(how-kahn)* . . . . good-looking 好 _____
☐ **hǎoyùn** *(how-yewn)* . . . . good luck *hao* _____

81

Don't forget that **Zhōngguó** dishes are regional and that various provinces have their own specialties. **Nǐ** won't want to miss out on the following specialties.

(tee-ahn) (jee-oh) (nee-ahng)
tián jiǔ niàng
sweet rice wine

(zwong-zr)
zòngzi
stuffed sweet rice wrapped
with bamboo leaves

(ssee-ah-roh) (hoon) (toon)
xiāròu hún tūn
shrimp and vegetables in a wrapper, boiled

(tahng-yew-ahn)
tāngyúan
sweet rice-flour ball

(choon-jyew-ahnr)
chūnjuǎnr
pastry filled with a savory mixture of
vegetables and meat (a spring roll)

After completing your meal, call the **fúwùyúan** and **gěi qían** just as **nǐ** learned in Step 16:

(cheeng) (gay)   (jahng-dahnr)
Qǐng gěi wǒ zhàngdānr.
please   give   bill

Below is a sample *(tsi-dahn)* **càidān** to help you prepare for your trip.
menu

JĪN HǍI
FÀNGUǍNR

CÀIDĀN

LĚNGPÁN (cold dishes)

	Yúan
báiqièjī (cold chicken)	1.15
lǔyā (cold duck with soy sauce)	1.20
xūn yú (smoked fish)	1.50
yóu bào xiā (oil-fried shrimp)	1.75

TĀNG (soup)

xī hóngshì dàn tāng (tomato and egg soup)	1.25
yú tāng (fish soup)	1.50
dàn huā tāng (egg flower soup)	1.00

ZHŪRÒU (pork)

táng cù páigǔ (sweet-and-sour spareribs)	2.25
gānzhá zhūpái (dry-fried fillet of pork)	2.50
qīngjiāo ròu dīng (pork squares with pepper)	2.00
qīngcài ròu sī (shredded pork with vegetables)	1.95

NÍURÒU (beef)

níuròu yángcōng (fried shredded beef with onion)	2.25
gān biān níuròu (fried shredded beef)	2.45
chǎo níuròu (stir-fried beef)	2.85

YÚXIĀ (seafood)

zhá dàxiā (fried prawns)	3.25
qīng dòu xiā rén (fried shrimp with green peas)	3.00
chǎo xiā piàn (stir-fried sliced prawns)	3.15
táng cù húang yú (sweet-and-sour yellow fish)	3.25
qīngzhēng lǐyú (steamed carp)	3.45

FÀN (rice)

bái fàn (plain rice)	0.30
dàn chǎo fàn (fried rice with egg)	1.20
ròu sī chǎo fàn (fried rice with shredded pork)	1.45

MÌAN (noodles)

jī sī mìan (noodles with shredded chicken)	1.50
ròu sī mìan (noodles with shredded pork)	1.35
xiārén mìan (noodles with shrimp)	1.75
chǎo mìan (fried noodles)	1.00

YǏNLÌAO (beverages)

jiǔ (wine)	0.85
píjiǔ (beer)	0.65
júzishǔi (orange juice)	0.55
kùangqúanshǔi (mineral water)	0.45
kāfēi (coffee)	0.45
chá (tea)	0.45

☐ **chá** *(chah)* . . . . tea
☐ **chábēi** *(chah-bay)* . . . . teacup
☐ **chádǐan** *(chah-dee-ahn)* . . . . light meal
☐ **chágǔan** *(chah-gwahn)* . . . . teahouse
☐ **cháhùi** *(chah-hway)* . . . . tea party

茶
cha

Zài Zhōnggúo, *(zow-fahn)* **zăofàn** is a very simple meal. You can eat **zăofàn** in *(nee-duh)* **nĭde lŭgŭan** *(woo-zr)* **wūzi**
breakfast / your / room

or **yě kěyi** eat in the **shítáng. Zài lŭgŭan,** a western-style **zăofàn** is *(chahng-chahng)* **chángcháng** provided
dining room / often

(lew-kuh)
for **lŭkè.**
tourists

Zăofàn 1 ....2.75 yúan

júzishŭi

kāfēi hùoshì chá

(jee-ahn) (dahn)
jīan dàn
fried   eggs

(too-sr)   *(gwo-jee-ahng)*
tŭsī húangyóu gŭojìang
toast butter   jam

Zăofàn 2 ....2.95 yúan

júzishŭi

kāfēi hùoshì chá

(jee-ahn) (ssee-ahng-chahng)
jīan xīangcháng
fried   sausage

tŭsī húangyóu gŭojìang

Zăofàn 3 ....3.25 yúan

júzishŭi

(hwo-tway)
hŭotŭi
ham

jīan dàn

(my-pee-ahn)
màipìan
cereal
(ruh) (chee-ow-kuh-lee)
rè qĭaokèlì
hot   chocolate

(yeen-lee-ow)
Yĭnlìao
beverages

kāfēi.......................0.45 yúan

chá........................0.45 yúan

júzishŭi....................0.55 yúan

☐ **chájù** *(chah-jyew)*.................. tea set
☐ **cháshŭi** *(chah-shway)*............. drink (tea, etc.)
☐ **cháyè** *(chah-yeh)*.................. tea leaf
☐ **hóngchá** *(hohng-chah)*.............. black tea
☐ **lŭchá** *(lew-chah)*.................. green tea

茶
cha

_____
_____
_____
_____

(dee-ahn-hwah)
Dìanhùa
telephone

Zài Zhōnggúo, what is different about the **dìanhùa?** *(dee-ahn-hwah)* telephone Well, **nǐ** never notice such things

until **nǐ** want to use them. **Dìanhùa** allow you to **dìng** *(deeng)* make **fángjian** *(fahng-jee-ahn)* reservations in a **lǔgǔan, mǎi** *(my)* buy

xìpìao *(ssee-pee-ow)* theater tickets **hé** *(huh)* and **fēijipìao,** *(fay-jee-pee-ow)* airplane tickets contact **nǐde** *(nee-duh)* your **péngyou,** *(pung-yoh)* friends check on the hours of a **bówùgǔan,** *(bwo-woo-gwahn)* museum

call a **chūzūchē,** *(choo-zoo-chuh)* taxi make emergency calls and a lot of other things that **wǒmen** need

to do **tiāntian.** *(tee-ahn-tee-ahn)* every day

Zài Zhōnggúo, jiālǐ *(jee-ah-lee)* homes **bù** not **cháng** *(chahng)* often **yǒu** *(yoh)* have **dìanhùa. Zài yóujú** *(yoh-jyew)* post office **yǒu** *(yoh)* there are **gōnggòng** *(goong-goong)* public **dìanhùa.** Also, **zài**

Zhōnggúo, most streets have a **jiēdào** *(jee-eh-dow)* street/subdistrict **bàngōngshì** *(bahn-goong-shr)* office in which you will **yě** *(yeh)* also find a **gōnggòng**

dìanhùa. Some **fēijichǎng** *(fay-jee-chahng)* airports **hé** a few of the large shopping centers have **dìanhùa tíng.** *(teeng)* telephone booths

Zhè shì Zhōnggúode dìanhùa.

The **dìanhùa tíng** *(teeng)* booths **xìang** *(ssee-ahng)* resemble those in **Měigúo** but,

as **nǐ** will see, there are some differences. This

is one of those moments when **nǐ** realize,

Wǒ bú zài Měigúo.

So let's learn how to operate the **dìanhùa.**

To make a **běndì** *(buhn-dee)* local **dìanhùa,** *(dee-ahn-hwah)* telephone call **nǐ** need to first

pay the **rén** *(ruhn)* person in the **jiēdào** *(jee-eh-dow)* subdistrict **bàngōngshì** *(bahn-goong-shr)* office or

the **rén** attending the **dìanhùa tíng.** *(teeng)* booth In a few

of the **dìanhùa tíng,** you can insert **qían** in a

coin box.

If **nǐ** want to make a **chángtú dìanhùa,** *(chahng-too)* *long-distance* you may place it through your **lǔgǔan**

service desk. **Nǐ** will be asked to fill out a form like the one **xìabìanr,** stating to whom

you are making the **dìanhùa** and to what **gúo.** *(gwo)* *country*

TELEPHONE CALL THROUGH PUBLIC BOOTH

No. 公用电话挂号单 Date

收电地址 Destination	
用户电话号码 Sender's no.	
收电人电话号码 Receiver's no.	
发电人姓名 Sender's name	
发电人地址 Address	
转帐号码 Transferred account no.	

以 下 由 工 作 人 员 填 写
The following will be completed by the operator.

挂 号 时 刻		通报完毕时刻	
通报报出时刻		通报开始时刻	
附 加 费		计费分钟数	
营业员代号 值机员代号		报 费	

Just to keep you on your toes, here's a fast review quiz of telephone **cí.** We've added

one—"telephone book," which translates literally as "telephone register." Can you guess

it? Draw **xìan** between the **Zhōngwén cí** and the **Yīngwén cí.**

(dee-ahn-hwah)
dìanhùa   telephone booth

(goong-goong)
gōnggòng dìanhùa   telephone book

(chahng-too)
chángtú dìanhùa   to make a telephone call

(teeng)
dìanhùa tīng   local telephone call

(boo)
dìanhùa bù   telephone

(dah)
dǎ dìanhùa   public telephone

(buhn-dee)
běndì dìanhùa   long-distance telephone call

So **xiànzài nǐ zhīdào** how **dǎ** *(jr-dow)* *(dah)* **dìanhùa** *(dee-ahn-hwah)*. But what do **nǐ shūo** *(shwo)* when **nǐ** finally get through to your party? The **rén** who answers the **dìanhùa** will usually say "**Wèi**" *(way)* when **tā** picks up the **tīngtǒng** *(teeng-twong)*. **Nǐ** should identify yourself by giving your **míngzi** and then by asking for the **rén** you wish to speak with: **Wǒ kěyǐ** *(kuh-yee)* **gēn Mǎlì** *(guhn)* **shūohùa ma?** *(shwo-hwah)*

Dìanhùa customs are not always the same from country to country. If **nǐ** are told "**Zhànxìan,**" *(jahn-ssee-ahn)* it simply means that the line is busy. And although it means "See you again," **Zhōngguó rén** usually say "**Zài jìan**" *(zi)* *(jee-ahn)* when they are ending a **dìanhùade** *(dee-ahn-hwah-duh)* **dùihùa** *(dway-hwah)*.
telephone   conversation

Xìanzài zhèr *(juhr)* **yǒu** *(yoh)* some sample **dùihùa** *(dway-hwah)*. Write them in the blanks **xìabīanr** *(ssee-ah-bee-ahnr)*.
here are   conversations   below

Nǐ shì *(shr)* **hǔochē** *(hwo-chuh)* **zhàn** *(jahn)* **ma?** _____
are   train   station

Nǐ shì bówùgǔan *(bwo-woo-gwahn)* **ma?** _Nǐ shì bówùgǔan ma?_
museum

Nǐ shì Jīn Hǎi *(jeen)* *(hi)* **Fàngǔanr ma?** _____
golden sea

Nǐ shì Běijīng Lǚgǔan ma? _____

Nǐ shì yóujú *(yoh-jyew)* **ma?** _____
post office

Nǎr *(nahr)* **yǒu** *(yoh)* **gōnggòng** *(goong-goong)* **dìanhùa?** _____
where is public

Nǎr yǒu dìanhùa bù? *(boo)* _____
book

Wǒde *(wo-duh)* **dìanhùa shì 765-8974.** _____
my

Nǐde *(nee-duh)* **dìanhùa dūoshǎo hǎo?** *(how)* _____
your   number

86 **Zhèr yǒu** another possible **dùihùa**. Listen to the **cí** and how they are used.

Christina:	**Wèi.** *(way)* hello **Wǒ shì Christina.**	**Lǐ sì tóngzhì zài ma?** comrade in	**Wǒ kěyǐ gēn tā** *(kuh-yee)(guhn)* may with	

Christina: **Wèi.** *(way)* hello **Wǒ shì Christina.** **Lǐ sì tóngzhì zài ma?** comrade in **Wǒ kěyǐ gēn tā** *(kuh-yee)(guhn)* may with
shūohùa ma? *(shwo-hwah)* speak

Operator: **Zhànxìan.** *(jahn-ssee-ahn)* the line is busy

Christina: **Wǒ zhǐ hùi shūo yìdǐanr Zhōngwén.** *(jr)* only *(yee-dee-ahnr)* a little **Qǐng nǐ màn yìdǐanr shūo.** *(cheeng)* please *(mahn)* slowly **Hǎo ma?** *(how)* okay

Operator: **Dùibùqǐ.** *(dway-boo-chee)* excuse me **Zhànxìan.**

Christina: **Xìexie.** *(ssee-eh-ssee-eh)* thanks **Zài jìan.** *(zi)* *(jee-ahn)*

Here is another possible **dùihùa.** *(dway-hwah)* conversation

Thomas: **Wǒ xǐang yào gěi Zhāng sān yīshēng dǎ dìanhùa.** *(gay)* give *(yee-shung)* doctor **Qǐng nǐ gàosu** *(gow-soo)* tell
wǒ tāde dìanhùa shì dūoshǎo. *(wo)* me *(tah-duh)* his *(dwo-show)* is

Dìanhùa fúwùyúan: **Tāde dìanhùa shì 827-3624.**

Thomas: **Dùibùqǐ. Qǐng nǐ zài shūo.** repeat

Dìanhùa fúwùyúan: **Tāde dìanhùa shì 827-3624.**

Thomas: **Xìexie. Zài jìan.**

Xìanzài nǐ are ready to use any **dìanhùa** in **Zhōnggúo.** Just take it **màn** *(mahn)* slowly and speak clearly.

Don't forget **nǐ néng wèn. . .** *(nung)* can *(wuhn)* ask

Běndì *(buhn-dee)* local **dìanhùa** *(dwo-show)* telephone call **dūoshǎo** how much **qían?** *(chee-ahn)* money *Běndì dìanhùa dūoshǎo qían?*

Dǎ *(dah)* make **dìanhùa dào** *(dow)* to **Běijīng dūoshǎo qían?** _____

Dǎ chángtú *(chahng-too)* long-distance **dìanhùa dào Měigúo dūoshǎo qían?** _____

Dǎ chángtú dìanhùa dào Rìběn *(rr-buhn)* Japan **dūoshǎo qían?** _____

Don't forget that **nǐ xūyào** *(ssee-yew-yow)* need change for the **dìanhùa!**

87

Step 20

Zài Zhōngguó, dìxiàtiedàochē *(dee-ssee-ah-tee-eh-dow-chuh)* means "underground road vehicle," or subway. There

is one **dìxiàtiedàochē** *(dee-ssee-ah-tee-eh-dow-chuh)* in **Běijīng** *(bay-jeeng)* but it is **bú tài cháng** *(boo) (ti) (chahng)*. Most **Zhōngguó rén** travel
Beijing   not too long

by **dìanchē** *(dee-ahn-chuh)* **hùoshì gōngòngqìchē** *(goong-goong-chee-chuh)*. **Zài Zhōngguó, gōngòngqìchē** are **chángchǎng** *(chahng-chahng)* very
trolley   bus   often

crowded. But **Zhōngguó rén** are very courteous to foreigners and it is not unusual

for a **lǔkè** to be offered a seat by a **Zhōngguó rén**. Let's learn how to take the

(goong-goong-chee-chuh)   *(dee-ssee-ah-tee-eh-dow-chuh)*   *(dee-ahn-chuh)*
gōngòngqìchē, dìxiàtiedàochē hùoshì dìanchē. Practice the following **cí** by saying them

aloud and by writing them in the blanks **xìabìanr.**

(dee-ssee-ah-tee-eh-dow-chuh)   *(dee-ahn-chuh)*   *(goong-goong-chee-chuh)*
dìxiàtiedàochē   **dìanchē**   **gōngòngqìchē**

_____   *dìanchē*   _____

(chuh) (jahn)
chē zhàn = (vehicle) stop _____

(loo)
lǔ = route _____

(sr-jee)
sījī = driver _____

(shoh-pee-ow-yew-ahn)
shòupìaoyúan = conductor _____

Let's also review the "transportation" **dòngcí** *(dwong-tsr)* at this point.

(shahng) (chuh)
shàng chē = to board
on   (vehicle)

(ssee-ah) (chuh)
xìa chē = to disembark
down   (vehicle)

_____   _____

(hwahn) (chuh)
hùan chē = to transfer
(vehicle)

(lew-sseeng)
lǔxíng = to travel

_____   *lǔxíng*

(dee-too)
Dìtú displaying the various **chē zhàn hé lù** are available at most major stops. Be sure
maps   *(chuh) (jahn)   (loo)*
                                  stops   routes

(shoh-pee-ow-yew-ahn)
to let the **shòupìaoyúan** know where you are going, because ticket prices are based on
conductor

(goong-goong-chee-chuh)   *(dee-ahn-chuh)*
distances traveled. This applies to both **gōnggòngqìchē** and **dìanchē**. **Xìabìanr** is a
bus   trolley

(dee-too)
dìtú that shows several places you may want to travel to by **gōnggòngqìchē** or **dìanchē**
map

(shoh-pee-ow-yew-ahn)
in any **Zhōngguó** city. Practice the **cí** by repeating them aloud so the **shòupìaoyúan** will
conductor

know exactly what you mean when you tell him or her where you are going.

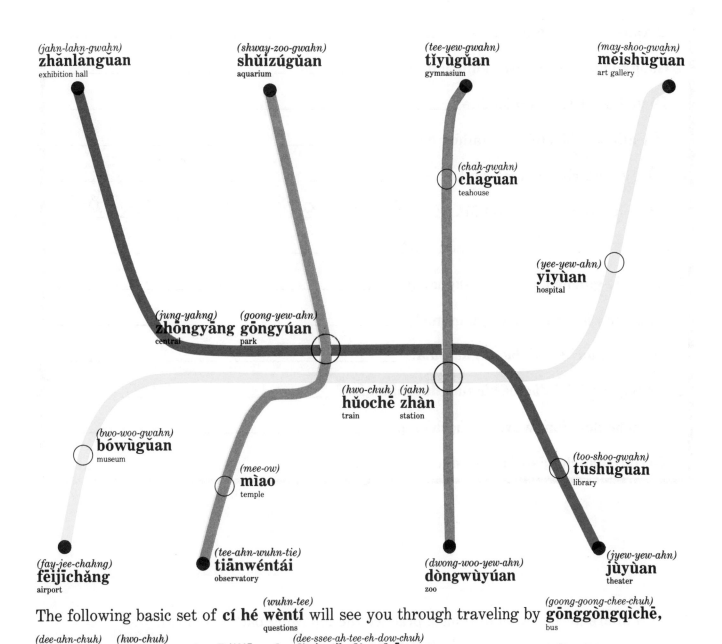

(jahn-lahn-gwahn)
zhǎnlǎnguǎn
exhibition hall

(shway-zoo-gwahn)
shǔizúguǎn
aquarium

(tee-yew-gwahn)
tǐyùguǎn
gymnasium

(may-shoo-gwahn)
meishǔguǎn
art gallery

(chah-gwahn)
cháguǎn
teahouse

(yee-yew-ahn)
yīyùan
hospital

(jung-yahng)
zhōngyǎng
central

(goong-yew-ahn)
gōngyúan
park

(hwo-chuh)
hǔochē
train

(jahn)
zhàn
station

(bwo-woo-gwahn)
bówùguǎn
museum

(too-shoo-gwahn)
túshǔguǎn
library

(mee-ow)
mìao
temple

(fay-jee-chahng)
fēijichǎng
airport

(tee-ahn-wuhn-tie)
tiānwéntái
observatory

(dwong-woo-yew-ahn)
dòngwùyúan
zoo

(jyew-yew-ahn)
jùyùan
theater

(wuhn-tee)
The following basic set of **cí hé wèntí** will see you through traveling by **gōnggòngqìchē**,
questions   bus

(dee-ahn-chuh)   *(hwo-chuh)*   *(dee-ssee-ah-tee-eh-dow-chuh)*
dìanchē,   **hǔochē** or by **Běijīngde dìxìatiedàochē.**
trolley   train   subway

89

Naturally, the first **wèntí shì** "**nǎr.**" *(nahr)*

(nahr) (shr) (goong-goong-chee-chuh) *(jahn)*
Nǎr shì gōnggòngqìchē zhàn?
where is   bus   stop

(dee-ahn-chuh)(jahn)
Nǎr shì diànchē zhàn?
trolley stop

(dee-ssee-ah-tee-eh-dow-chuh) *(jahn)*
Nǎr shì dìxiàtiědàochē   zhàn?
subway   stop

Practice the following basic **wèntí** out loud and then **xiě** them in the blanks **zài yòubianr.** *(ssee-eh)* write *(zi) (yoh-bee-ahnr)* at

---

(goong-goong-chee-chuh) (jahn) (zi) (nahr)
1. **Gōnggongqìchē zhàn zài nǎr?**_____
bus   stop   is   where

(dee-ahn-chuh)
Diànchē zhàn zài nǎr?_____
trolley

(dee-ssee-ah-tee-eh-dow-chuh)
Dìxiàtiědàochē zhàn zài nǎr?_____
subway

2. **Gōnggòngqìchē shénme shíhòu dào?**_____
what   time   arrives *(shr-hoh) (dow)*

Diànchē shénme shíhòu dào?_____

Dìxiàtiědàochē shénme shíhòu dào?_____

3. **Gōnggòngqìchē shénme shíhòu kāi?**_____
what   time   leaves *(shr-hoh) (ki)*

Diànchē shénme shíhòu kāi? _*Diànchē shénme shíhòu kāi?*_

Dìxiàtiědàochē shénme shíhòu kāi?_____

4. **Gōnggòngqìchē kāi dào bówùguǎn ma?**_____
goes to   museum *(ki) (dow) (bwo-woo-gwahn)*

Diànchē kāi dào dòngwùyúan ma? _____
zoo *(dwong-woo-yew-ahn)*

Dìxiàtiědàochē kāi dào lǚguǎn ma? _____

5. **Gōnggòngqìchē dào bówùguǎn duōshǎo qián?**_____
to   how much   money *(dow) (dwo-show) (chee-ahn)*

Diànchē dào dòngwùyúan duōshǎo qían?_____

Dìxiàtiědàochē dào lǚguǎn duōshǎo qían?_____

Xìanzài nǐ are in the swing of things, practice the following patterns aloud,

substituting **gōnggōngqìchē** for **diànchē** and so on.
(goong-goong-chee-chuh) *(dee-ahn-chuh)*
bus   trolley

1. Zài nǎr mǎi *(my)* gōnggòngqìchē pìao *(pee-ow)*? Dìanchē pìao? Dìxìatǐedàochē pìao *(dee-see-ah-tee-eh-dow-chuh)*?
   buy   ticket   subway

2. Dào *(dow)* lǚgǔan, gōnggòngqìchē *(goong-goong-chee-chuh)* shénme shíhòu *(shr-hoh)* kāi? Dào bówùgǔan *(bwo-woo-gwahn)*, gōnggòngqìchē
   to   bus   what   time   leaves   museum

   shénme shíhòu kāi? Dào chágǔan *(chah-gwahn)*, gōnggòngqìchē shénme shíhòu kāi?
   teahouse

3. Qù *(chee-yew)* chágǔande *(chah-gwahn-duh)* gōnggòngqìchē zhàn *(jahn)* zài nǎr?
   to   teahouse's   stop

   Qù *(chee-yew)* tǐyùgǔande *(tee-yew-gwahn-duh)* dìanchē zhàn zài nǎr?
   to   gymnasium's

   Qù měishùgǔande *(may-shoo-gwahn-duh)* gōnggòngqìchē zhàn zài nǎr?
   art gallery

   Qù zhǎnlǎngǔande *(jahn-lahn-gwahn-duh)* dìanchē zhàn zài nǎr?
   exhibition hall's

   Qù yīyùande *(yee-yew-ahn-duh)* dìxìatǐedàochē zhàn zài nǎr?
   hospital's

   Qù dòngwùyúande *(dwong-woo-yew-ahn-duh)* gōnggòngqìchē zhàn zài nǎr?
   zoo's

   Qù zhōngyāng *(jung-yahng)* gōngyúande *(goong-yew-ahn-duh)* dìanchē zhàn zài nǎr?
   central   park's

   Qù bówùgǔande *(bwo-woo-gwahn-duh)* dìxìatǐedàochē zhàn zài nǎr?
   museum's

Nǐ kàn *(kahn)* the following dǐanxíngde dùihùa *(dee-ahng-ssee-duh)(dway-hwah)* and xǐe *(ssee-eh)* the dùihùa in the blanks zài yòubīanr *(yoh-bee-ahnr)*.
read   typical   conversations   write   right

Nǎ yí lù *(loo)* qù *(chee-yew)* dòngwùyúan *(dwong-woo-yew-ahn)*? _____
which (C) route to   zoo

Qí lù *(chee)*. _____
seven

Qí lù chē shénme shíhòu *(shr-hoh)* dào *(dow)*? _____
what   time   arrives

Shí fēn zhōng *(shr)(fuhn)*. _____
ten   minutes

Yào bú yào hùanchē *(yow)(boo)(hwahn-chuh)*? *yào bú yào hùanchē?*
must   transfer

Yào *(yow)*, zài zhōngyāng *(jung-yahng)* gōngyúan *(goong-yew-ahn)* hùanchē. _____
yes   central   park

Cóng *(tswong)* zhèr *(juhr)* dào *(dow)* dòngwùyúan yào *(yow)* dūoshǎo *(dwo-show)* shíjīan? _____
from   here   to   takes   how much

Yào èrshí *(yow)(ur-shr)* fēn zhōng. _____
takes   twenty

Pìao dūoshǎo qían *(pee-ow)*? _____
ticket

Yì máo qían. _____ 91

Nǐ néng translate the following thoughts into **Zhōngwén ma?** The answers **zài xiàbianr.**

1. Where is the bus stop?_____

2. How much does a ticket to Beijing cost? _____

3. What time does route seven arrive?_____

4. Where do I buy a ticket? _____

5. Where is the trolley stop? _____

6. I would like to get out._____

7. Must I transfer?_____

8. Where must I transfer?___*zài nǎr huànchē?*___

Zhèr shì another **sān ge dòngcí.**
(dwong-tsr)
(C)   verbs

(ssee)
xǐ = to wash

(dee-oh)
diū = to lose

(yow)
yào = to take (time)

_____   _____   _____

Nǐ zhīdào the way **dòngcí** work in **Zhōngwén,** so translate the following thoughts with
(jr-dow)
know

these **xīn dòngcí.** The answers **yě zài xiàbianr.**
(sseen)   *(yeh)*
new   also

1. I wash the jacket._____

2. You lose the book.___*Nǐ diūle shū.*_____

3. It takes 20 minutes to the museum._____

4. It takes three hours by car. _____

ANSWERS

4. Yào zuò sān gè zhōngtóu qìchē.	2. Nǐ diūle shū.
3. Yào èrshí fēn zhōng dào bówùguǎn.	1. Wǒ xǐ zhè shàngyī.
8. Zài nǎr huànchē?	4. Wǒ zài nǎr mǎi piào?
7. Yào bú yào huànchē?	3. Qī lù chē shénme shíhòu dào?
6. Wǒ xiǎng yào xiàchē.	2. Dào Běijīng duōshǎo qián?
5. Diànchē zhàn zài nǎr?	1. Gōnggòngqìchē zhàn zài nǎr?

92

Mǎi hé Mài
(my) buy *(my)* sell

Zài wàigúo, *(wi-gwo)* shopping is very **yǒuyìsi.** *(yoh-yee-sr)* The simple everyday task of buying **yì píng niúnǎi** *(peeng)* *(nee-oh-ni)*
foreign country interesting bottle milk

hùoshì yí ge pínggǔo *(peeng-gwo)* becomes a challenge that **nǐ xìanzài** should be able to meet quickly
(C) apple

and easily. Of course, **nǐ** will purchase **jìnìanpǐn,** *(jee-nee-ahn-peen)* **yóupìao hé míngxìnpian,** *(yoh-pee-ow)* *(meeng-sseen-pee-ahn)* but do not
souvenirs stamps postcards

forget those many other **dōngxi** *(dwong-ssee)* ranging from shoelaces to aspirin that **nǐ** might need
things

unexpectedly. **Nǐ zhīdào** *(jr-dow)* the difference between **yí ge shū dìan hé yí ge yào fáng ma?** *(shoo)* *(dee-ahn)* *(yow)* *(fahng)*
know (C) bookstore (C) pharmacy

Let's learn about the different **shāngdìan** *(shahng-dee-ahn)* in **Zhōnggúo.** **Xìabianr shì yí ge dìtú** *(dee-too)* of a
stores (C) map

typical **Zhōnggúo chéngshì.** *(chung-shr)*
city

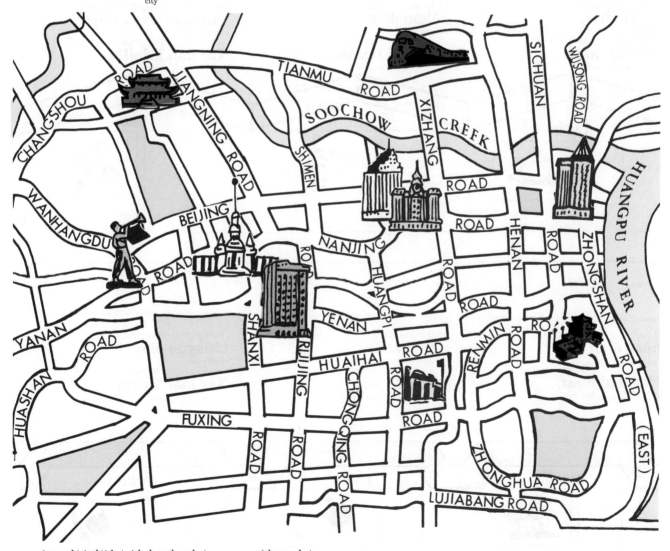

Zài xìa yè shì shāngdìan *(ssee-ah)* *(yeh)* *(shr)* *(shahng-dee-ahn)* in this **chéngshì.** *(chung-shr)* Be sure to fill in each blank below the
next pages are stores city

hùar with the **shāngdìande míngzi.** *(shahng-dee-ahn-duh)*
shop's

(mee-ahn-bow) (dee-ahn)
mìanbāo dìan
bakery
(my) (mee-ahn-bow)
Nàr mǎi mìanbāo.
there buy bread

(roh) (dee-ahn)
ròu dìan
butcher shop
(my) (roh)
Nàr mǎi ròu.
there buy meat

(ssee) (yee) (dee-ahn)
xǐ yī dìan
laundry
(ssee) (yee-foo)
Nàr xǐ yīfú.
wash clothes

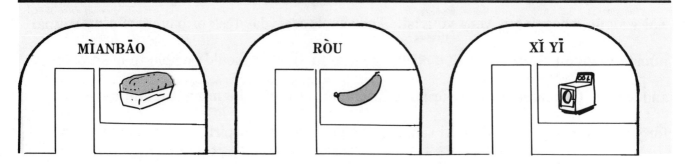

(kah-fay) (dee-ahn)
kāfēi dìan
coffeeshop
(huh) (kah-fay)
Nàr hē kāfēi.
drink coffee

(jah-hwo) (dee-ahn)
záhùo dìan
drugstore
(fay-zow)
Nàr mǎi féizào.
soap

(yow) (dee-ahn) (yow) (fahng)
yào dìan /yào fáng
pharmacy
(ah-sr-pee-leen)
Nàr mǎi āsīpílín.
aspirin

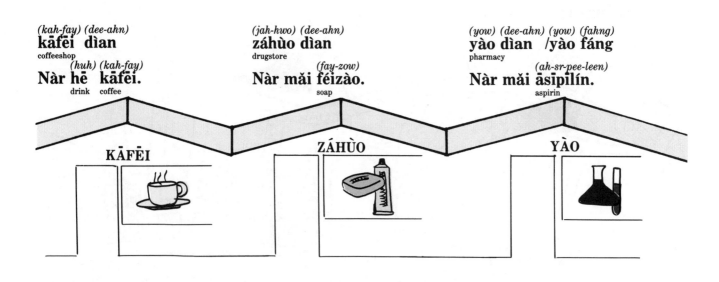

(hwar) (dee-ahn)
hūar dìan
flower shop
(hwar)
Nàr mǎi hūar.
flowers

(yahn) (dee-ahn)
yān dìan
tobacco store
(yahn)
Nàr mǎi yān.
tobacco

(tahng-gwo) (dee-ahn)
tánggǔo dìan
candy store
(tahng-gwo)
Nàr mǎi tánggǔo.
candy

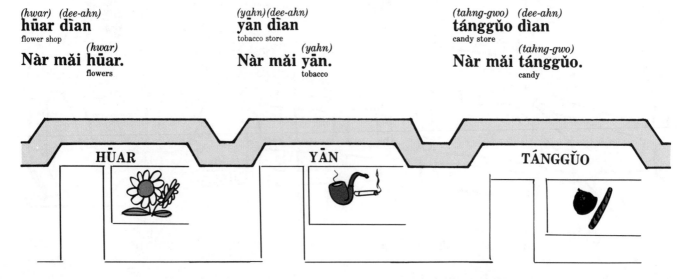

(nee-oh-ni) (dee-ahn)
níunǎi dìan
dairy
(nee-oh-ni)
Nàr mǎi níunǎi.
milk

(jow-ssee-ahng) (chee-tsi) (dee-ahn)
zhàoxìang qìcái dìan
camera store
(dee-pee-ahn)
Nàr mǎi dǐpìan.
film

(tsi) (dee-ahn)
cài dìan
vegetable store
(cheeng-tsi)
Nàr mǎi qīngcài.
fresh vegetables

NÍUNǍI   ZHÀOXÌANG QÌCÁI   CÀI

(teeng-chuh) (chahng)
tíngchē chǎng
parking lot
(teeng) (chuh)
Nàr tíng chē.
park   cars

(lee-fah) (dee-ahn)
lǐfà dìan
hairdresser's
(lee) (fah)
Nàr lǐ fà.
cut   hair

(tsi-fung) (dee-ahn)
cáiféng dìan
tailor's
(zwo) (yee-foo)
Nàr zùo yīfú.
make   clothes

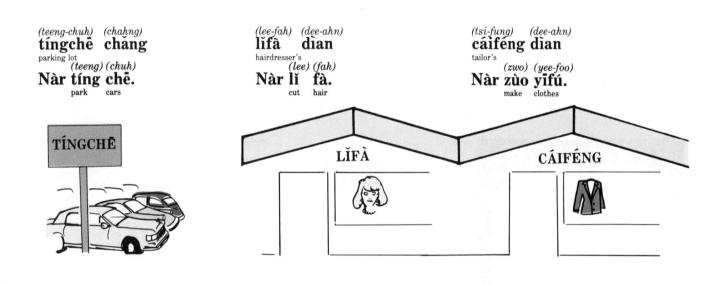

LǏFÀ   CÁIFÉNG

(yoh-jyew)
yóujú
post office
(yoh-pee-ow)
Nàr mǎi yóupìao.
stamps

(goo-dwong) (dee-ahn)
gǔdǒng dìan
antique store
(goo-dwong)
Nàr mǎi gǔdǒng.
antiques

(yeen-hahng)
yínháng
(hwahn-chee-ahn)
Nàr hùanqían.
exchange money

YÓUJÚ   GǓDǑNG   YÍNHÁNG

(shr-peen) (dee-ahn)
shípǐn dìan
grocery store
Nàr mǎi ròu, shǔiguǒ
(roh)   (shway-gwo)
meat   fruit
(nee-oh-ni)
hé níunǎi.
milk

(shoo-shr) (dee-ahn)
shúshí dìan
delicatessen
Nàr mǎi shúshí.
(shoo-shr)
cold cuts

(shway-gwo) (dee-ahn)
shǔiguǒ dìan
fruit store
Nàr mǎi shǔiguǒ.
(shway-gwo)
fruit

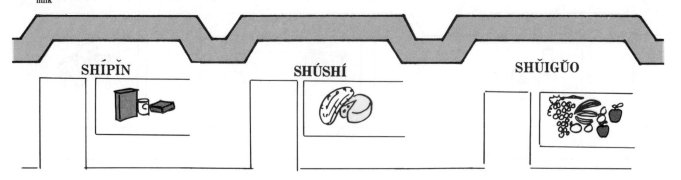

SHÍPǏN   SHÚSHÍ   SHǓIGUǑ

(dee-ahn-yeeng-yew-ahn)
dìanyǐngyùan
movie theater
(kahn) (dee-ahn-yeeng)
Nàr kàn dìanyǐng.
see   movie

(shoo-bow) (tahn)
shūbào tān
book stand
(bow-jr)   (zah-jr)
Nàr mǎi bàozhǐ, zázhì
newspapers magazines
(shoo)
hé shū.
books

(gahn-ssee) (dee-ahn)
gānxǐ dìan
dry cleaner's
(gahn-ssee) (yee-foo)
Nàr gānxǐ yīfú.
dry clean   clothes

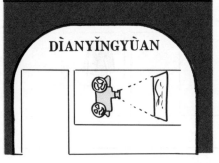

DÌANYǏNGYÙAN

SHŪBÀO

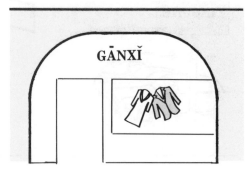

GĀNXǏ

(wuhn-jyew) (dee-ahn)
wénjù dìan
stationery store
(jr)
Nàr mǎi zhǐ.
paper

(shoo) (dee-ahn)
shū dìan
bookstore
(shoo)
Nàr mǎi shū.
books

(bi-hwo)   (dee-ahn)
bǎihùo dìan
department store
(rr-yong) (bi-hwo)
Nàr mǎi rìyòng bǎihùo.
everyday   things

(see Step 22)

WÉNJÙ   SHŪ   BǍIHÙO

(tsi-chahng)
càichǎng
market
(my) *(cheeng-tsi)*
Nàr mǎi qīngcài
buy   fresh vegetables
(shway-gwo)
hé shuǐguǒ.
fruit

(jee-nee-ahn-peen) *(dee-ahn)*
jìnìanpǐn dìan
souvenir   store
(jee-nee-ahn-peen)
Nàr mǎi jìnìanpǐn.
souvenirs

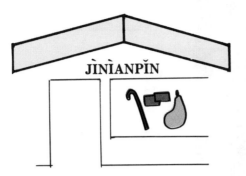

(jee-ah-yoh) *(jahn)*
jiayóu zhàn
gasoline   station
(chee-yoh)
Nàr mǎi qìyóu.
gasoline

(lew-sseeng) *(shuh)*
lǚxíng shè
travel   agency
(fay-jee-pee-ow)
Nàr mǎi fēijīpìao.
airplane ticket

(jung-bee-ow) *(dee-ahn)*
zhōngbǐao dìan
watchmaker's
(jung)
Nàr mǎi zhǒng
clocks
(bee-ow)
hé bǐao.
watches

(yew) *(dee-ahn)*
yú dìan
fish   store
(yew)
Nàr mǎi yú.
fish

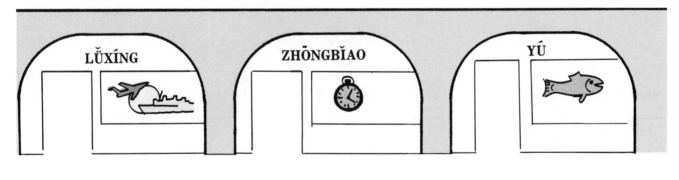

(shahng-dee-ahn) *(shun-muh)* *(shr-hoh)* *(ki)*
Zài Zhōngguó, shāngdìan shénme shíhou kāi? Normally, **shāngdìan** are open **qī tīan** per
shops   what   time   open
(chee)(tee-ahn)
seven days
(sseeng-chee) *(shahng-woo)* *(jee-oh)* *(dee-ahn)* *(dow)* *(ssee-ah-woo)* *(lee-oh)* *(dee-ahn)*
xīngqī from **shàngwǔ jǐu dǐan dào xìawǔ lìu dǐan.** Of course, **shíjīanbiao** vary from
week   morning   nine   o'clock   to   afternoon   six   o'clock
(shr-jee-ahn-bee-ow)
hours

shāngdìan to **shāngdìan.** Usually, **shāngdìan** remain open during the lunch hour and, on

(sseeng-chee-tee-ahn)
xīngqītian, most **shāngdìan** extend their shopping hours.
Sundays

Is there anything else that makes **Zhōngguó shāngdìan** different from **Měiguó**

shāngdìan? To find out, look at the **hùar** on the following **yè.**
(yeh)
page

97

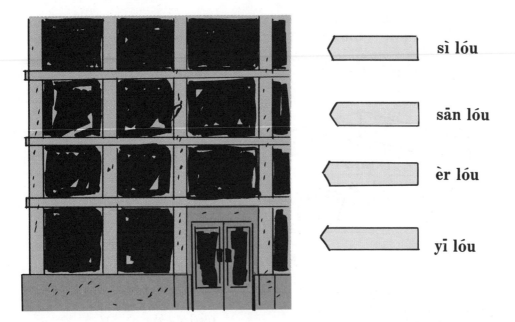

sì lóu

sān lóu

èr lóu

yī lóu

Contrary to European custom, where the first floor is called the ground floor, in **Zhōngguó**

(and in **Měiguó),** the first floor is exactly what it says! **Xìanzài** that **nǐ** know the

(meeng-zr)
míngzi for **Zhōngguó shāngdìan,** let's practice shopping.
names
(shahng-dee-ahn)
stores

I.   First step — **Nǎr?**

(nee-oh-ni) (dee-ahn)(zi) (nahr)
Níunǎi dìan zài nǎr?
dairy   is   where

(yeen-hahng)
Yínháng zài nǎr?
bank

(dee-ahn-yeeng-yew-ahn)
Dìanyǐngyùan zài nǎr?
movie theater

(shahng-dee-ahn)
Go through the **shāngdìan** introduced in this step and ask **"nǎr"** with each **shāngdìan.**
stores

Another way of asking **"nǎr"** is to say

(foo-jeen) (yoh)
Fùjìn yǒu níunǎi dìan ma?
vicinity   has

(foo-jeen) (yeen-hahng)
Fùjìn yǒu yínháng ma?
vicinity   bank

Go through the **shāngdìan** again using this new **wèntí.**

II.   Next step — tell them what **nǐ xūyào hùoshì xiǎng yào.**
(ssee-yew-yow)   *(ssee-ahng) (yow)*
need   would   like

(ssee-yew-yow)
1) **Wǒ xūyào . . .**   _Wǒ xūyào_ _____
need

(yoh)
2) **Nǐmen yǒu . . . ma?** _____
you   have

(ssee-ahng) (yow)
98   3) **Wǒ xiǎng yào . . .** _____
would like

Wǒ xūyào yí ge pínggǔo.
(ssee-yew-yow) *(peeng-gwo)*
need (C) apple

Nǐmen yǒu pínggǔo ma?
(yoh)
you have

Wǒ xiǎng yào yí ge pínggǔo.
(ssee-ahng) *(yow)*
would like (C)

Wǒ xūyào yì píng kùangqúanshuǐ.
(peeng) *(kwahng-chyew-ahn-shway)*
bottle mineral water

Nǐmen yǒu kùangqúanshuǐ ma?
(kwahng-chyew-ahn-shway)
mineral water

Wǒ xiǎng yào yì píng kùangqúanshuǐ.
(peeng) *(kwahng-chyew-ahn-shway)*
bottle mineral water

Go through the glossary at the end of this **shū** and select **èrshí ge cí.** Drill the above *(ur-shr)*
twenty (C)

patterns with **zhè èrshí ge cí.** Don't cheat. Drill them **jīntiān.** **Xìanzài,** take **èrshí** *(jeen-tee-ahn)*
(C) today

ge cí more from **nǐde zìdiǎn** and do the same. And don't just drill them **jīntiān.** *(zr-dee-ahn)*
(C) dictionary

Take more **cí míngtīan** and drill them also. *(meeng-tee-ahn)*
tomorrow

III. Next step — find out **dūoshǎo qían.**
(dwo-show) *(chee-ahn)*
how much money

Nà ge dūoshǎo qían? _____
(nah) *(dwo-show)* *(chee-ahn)*
that (C) how much

Qianbǐ dūoshǎo qían?
(chee-ahn-bee)
pencil

Míngxìnpìan dūoshǎo qían?
(meeng-sseen-pee-ahn)
postcard

Yóupìao dūoshǎo qían?
(yoh-pee-ow)
stamp

Pínggǔo dūoshǎo qían?
(peeng-gwo)
apple

Júzi dūoshǎo qían?
(jyew-zr)
orange

Kùangqúanshuǐ dūoshǎo qían?
(kwahng-chyew-ahn-shway)
mineral water

Using these same **cí** that **nǐ** selected **shàngbīanr, yě** drill these **wèntí.**
(shahng-bee-ahnr) *(yeh)*
above also

IV. If **nǐ bù zhīdào** where to find something, **nǐ wèn**
(boo) *(jr-dow)* *(wuhn)*
don't know ask

Nǎr mǎi āsīpílín?
(my) *(ah-sr-pee-leen)*
buy aspirin

Zài nǎr mǎi tàiyáng yǎnjìng?
(ti-yahng) *(yahn-jeeng)*
sun glasses

Once **nǐ zhīdào** what **nǐ** want, **nǐ shūo,**
(jr-dow) *(shwo)*
know say

Wǒ xiǎng yào zhè ge.
(juh) *(guh)*
this (C)

Hùoshì, if **nǐ** don't want something, **nǐ shūo,**

Wǒ bù xǐhuan nà ge.
(boo) *(ssee-hoo-ahn)* *(nah)*
not like that (C)

Xìanzài nǐ are all set to shop for anything!

99

Step 22

(bi-hwo) (dee-ahn)
Bǎihùo Dìan
department   store

At this point, **nǐ** should just about be ready for **nǐde Zhōngguó lǚxíng.** **Nǐ** have gone

shopping for those last-minute odds 'n ends. Most likely, the store directory at your

(bi-hwo) (dee-ahn)   (ssee-ah-bee-ahnr-duh)   (jr-dow) (huhn) (dwo)
local **bǎihùo dìan** does not look like the one **xìabianrde.** **Nǐ** already **zhīdào hěn dūo**
department store   below   know   very   many

cí and **nǐ** can guess at others. **Nǐ zhīdào "nürén" shì Zhōngwén** for women, so if **nǐ**

(ssee-yew-yow)   (loh)
xūyào something for a **nürén, nǐ** would probably look on the **sān** or **èr lóu.**
need   floor

7. LÓU	mìanbāo shítáng shúshí yǐnlìao	jīyǎ shǔigǔo qīngcài	wàigúo shípǐn jǐu yěwèi ròu lèi
6. LÓU	chúang tǎnzi he bèi sùlìao pǐn	jīajù dēng dōngfāng hùo	dìtǎn hūar
5. LÓU	yínqì dìanqì pǐn bōli	jīatíng yòngpǐn shìhào yòngpǐn chúfáng jīajù	sǔo táoqì cíqì
4. LÓU	shū dìanshì értóng jīajù yīngér yòngpǐn	wánjù yùeqì shōuyīnjī wénjù chàngpīan	yān zázhì bàozhǐ
3. LÓU	záhùo nǚrén yīfú	nánrén yīfú nǚrén màozi	shìwù zhāolǐng gùkè fúwù
2. LÓU	qìchē yòngpǐn nǚrén nèiyīkù shǒujùanr	yùshì yòngpǐn xíe gōngjù	chúangdān yùndòng yòngpǐn
1. LÓU	zhàoxìang yòngpǐn nánrén màozi sǎn zhūbǎo	shǒutàor pízhìpǐn wàzi zhōngbǐao	nánrén yòngpǐn xīangshǔi tánggǔo

(yee-foo)   (hi)
Let's start a checklist for **nǐde lǚxíng.** Besides **yīfú, nǐ hǎi xūyào shénme?**
clothing   still need   what

(yeeng-gi) (nah)
For your trip, **nǐ yīnggāi ná shénme?**
should   take

100

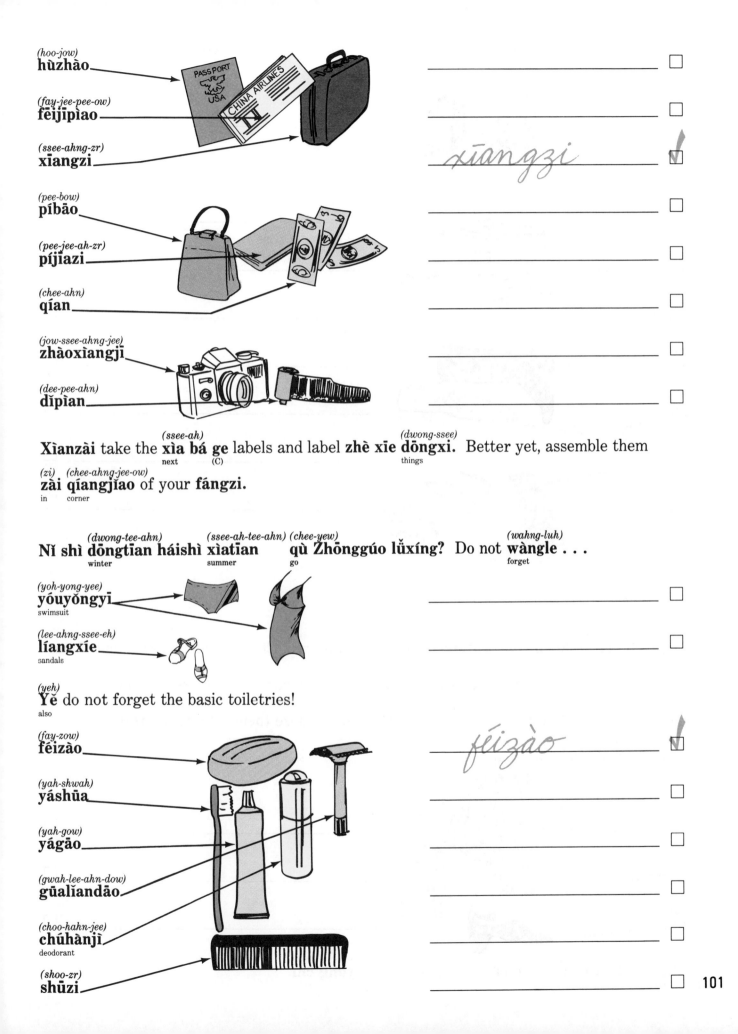

(hoo-jow)
hùzhào □

(fay-jee-pee-ow)
fēijīpiào □

(ssee-ahng-zr)
xiāngzi ☑ *xiāngzi*

(pee-bow)
píbāo □

(pee-jee-ah-zr)
píjiāzi □

(chee-ahn)
qían □

(jow-ssee-ahng-jee)
zhàoxiàngjī □

(dee-pee-ahn)
dǐpìan □

Xìanzài take the **xìa bá ge** labels and label **zhè xīe dōngxi.** Better yet, assemble them
next (C) things

(zi) *(chee-ahng-jee-ow)*
zài qiángjǐao of your **fángzi.**
in corner

(dwong-tee-ahn) *(ssee-ah-tee-ahn)* *(chee-yew)* *(wahng-luh)*
Nǐ shì dōngtīan háishì xìatīan **qù Zhōnggúo lǚxíng?** Do not **wàngle . . .**
winter summer go forget

(yoh-yong-yee)
yóuyǒngyī □
swimsuit

(lee-ahng-ssee-eh)
líangxíe □
sandals

(yeh)
Yě do not forget the basic toiletries!
also

(fay-zow)
féizào ☑ *féizào*

(yah-shwah)
yáshūa □

(yah-gow)
yágāo □

(gwah-lee-ahn-dow)
gūalǐandāo □

(choo-hahn-jee)
chúhànjì □
deodorant

(shoo-zr)
shūzi □

For the rest of the **dōngxi**, let's start with the outside layers and work our way in.

(wi-yee)
wàiyī _____ ☑

(yew-yee)
yǔyī _____ ☐

(sahn)
sǎn _____ ☐

(shoh-towr)
shǒutàor _____ ☐

(mow-zr)
màozi _____ ☐

(ssee-yew-eh-zr)
xūezi _____ ☐

(ssee-eh)
xie _____ ☐

(wah-zr)
wàzi _____ ☐

(koo-wah)
kùwà _____ ☐

Take the **xìa** *(ssee-ah)* **shíwu ge** *(shr-woo)* labels and label **zhè xīe dōngxi.** *(dwong-ssee)* Check and make sure that **tāmen**
_{next}   _{fifteen}   _(C)   _{things}

are clean and ready for **nǐde lǚxíng.** Be sure to do the same with the rest of the

dōngxi nǐ pack. Check them off on this list as **nǐ** organize them. **Cóng xìanzài** on, **nǐ** *(tswong)*
_{from} _{now}

yǒu "**féizào**" and not "soap." *(yoh)* *(fay-zow)*
_{have}

(shway-yee)
shùiyī _____ ☐

(shway-pow)
shùipáo _____ ☐

(two-ssee-eh)
tūoxíe _____ ☐

(shway-pow) *(two-ssee-eh)* *(yoh-yong)* *(chr)*
Shùipáo hé tūoxíe can double for **nǐ** at the **yóuyǒng chí.**
102 _{bathrobe}   _{slippers}   _{swimming}   _{pool}

(ssee-jwahng)
xīzhuāng ☐

(leeng-di)
lǐngdài ☐

(shoh-jyew-ahnr)
shǒujùanr ☐

(chun-yee)
chènyī *chènyī* ☐

(shahng-yee)
shàngyī ☐

(koo-zr)
kùzi ✓

(lee-ahn-yee-chyewn)
líanyīqún ☐

(chun-yee)
chènyī ☐

(chyewn-zr)
qúnzi ☐

(mow-yee)
máoyī ☐

(ssee-wong-jow)
xiongzhào ☐

(chun-chyewn)
chènqún ☐

(nay-koo)
nèikù ☐

(nay-yee)
nèiyī ☐

Xìanzài, nǐ are **yùbèi hǎo le** for your **lǚxíng.** The next step will give **nǐ** a quick
(yew-bay)(how)
prepared   well

introduction to some of the signs that **nǐ** will see while **nǐ** are in **Zhōngguó.** They will help

nǐ in your **lǚxíng.** Following the signs is a Chinese-English and English-Chinese glossary.

Refer to it when **nǐ** need help with any unfamiliar **cí.** Then **nǐ** are off to the **fēijīchǎng.**
(fay-jee-chahng)
airport

(yee-loo-peeng-ahn)
Yílùpíngān!
safe and peaceful journey

Step 23

小 心 = **Caution**

Zhèr shì some of the most important **Zhōngguó** signs. **Xíaoxin!** *(ssee-ow-sseen)*
be careful

热 — Hot

冷 — Cold

推 — Push

拉 — Pull

入口 — Entrance

出口 — Exit

闲人免进 — No entrance

空 — Vacant

出租 — For hire; for rent

出售 — For sale

关闭 — Closed

占用 — Occupied

客满 — Sold out

已预定 — Reserved

禁止摄影 — No photos allowed

危险 — Danger

停止 — Stop

GLOSSARY
Chinese-English

A

ǎi .... short
āsīpǐlín .... aspirin

B

bā .... eight
bǎ .... (C)
bái .... white
bǎi .... hundred
bǎihùo .... things
bǎihùo dìan .... department store
báitīan .... daytime
bàn .... half
bàng .... pound
bàngōngshì .... office
báo .... thin
bāogǔo .... parcel
bàozhǐ .... newspaper
bāshí .... eighty
báyùe .... August
bēi .... glass, cup
běi .... north
bèi .... quilt
běibīanr .... North
běifāng .... northern
Běijīng .... Beijing
běn .... bound together
běndì dìanhùa ..... local telephone call
bǐ .... writing instrument
bīanr .... side
bīao .... form, schedule, watch
bīaogé .... form, schedule
bīng .... ice
bìng .... sick
bīng dīan .... freezing point
bīngxīang .... refrigerator
bōli, bōlibēi .... glass
bówùgǔan .... museum
bù .... not, department
bú .... not
bùhǎo, bù hǎo
.... not good, bad; not well, badly

C

cài .... dish, vegetable
càichǎng .... market
càidān .... menu
cài dìan .... vegetable store
cáiféng dìan .... tailor's
cānchē .... dining car
cānjīn .... napkin
cǎo .... grass
cèsǔo .... lavatory
chá .... tea
chà .... before, lacking
chábēi .... teacup
chàbùdǔo .... about
chágǔan .... teahouse
cháng .... long
cháng, chángcháng .... often
chàngpīan .... record
chángtú dìanhùa
.... long-distance telephone call
chǎo .... stir-fried
chà yí kè .... quarter to
chāzi .... fork

C (column 2)

chē .... vehicle, car
chēfáng .... garage
chéngshì .... city
chènqún .... slip
chènyī .... shirt, blouse
chēxīang .... compartment
chē zhàn .... (vehicle) stop
chí .... pool
chī .... to eat
chīfàn .... to eat a meal
chōuyān .... to smoke
chū .... out
chúan .... boat
chúang .... bed
chūanghù .... window
chūanglían .... curtain
chúfáng .... kitchen
chúhànjì .... deodorant
chūkǒu .... exit
chūntīan .... spring
chūzuchē .... taxi
cí .... word
cíqì .... porcelain
cóng .... from

D

dà .... big
dǎ ... to make (telephone call, telegram)
dǎ .... to travel, by
dàdào .... boulevard
dài .... to bring
dǎkāi .... to open
dàlù .... mainland
dàn .... egg
dānchéng .... one-way
dānzi .... slip of paper
dào .... to arrive, to
dāozi .... knife
dàxīao .... size
Dégúo .... Germany
dēng .... light
Déwén .... German
dī .... low
dǐan .... o'clock
dìan .... store, shop, electricity
dìanbào .... telegram
dìanchē .... trolley
dìanhùa ... telephone, telephone call
dìanhùa bù .... telephone book
dìanhùa tíng .... telephone booth
dìanqì pǐn .... electrical goods
dìanshì .... television
dǐanxīn .... pastry
dǐanxíng .... typical
dìanyǐng .... movie
dìanyǐngyùan .... movie theater
dìbā .... eighth
dìfāng .... place
dìng .... to book, to reserve
dǐpìan .... film
dìqī .... seventh
dìtǎn .... carpet
dìtú .... map
dīu .... to lose
dìxìashì .... basement
dìxìatiedàochē .... subway
dǒng .... to understand

D (column 3)

dōng .... east
dōngbīanr .... East
dòngcí .... verb
dōngfāng .... eastern, oriental
dōngfāng hùo .... oriental goods
dōngtīan .... winter
dòngwùyúan .... zoo
dōngxi .... thing
dōngyáng .... east ocean, Japan
dōu .... all
dòu .... bean
dù .... degree
dǔan .... short
dùibùqǐ .... excuse me
dùihùa .... conversation
dùihùan chù .... money-exchange office
dǔo .... many, much
dǔoshǎo .... how much?

E

è .... hungry
èr .... two
èr děng .... second-class
èrshí .... twenty
èryùe .... February
érzi .... son

F

Fǎgúo .... France
fàn .... meal, rice
fáng .... room, apartment
fāngfǎ .... ways
fángjīan .... room
fàngǔanr .... restaurant
fángzi .... house
fàntīng .... dining room
Fǎwén .... French
fēi .... to fly
fēijī .... airplane
fēijīchǎng .... airport
fēijīpìao .... airplane ticket
féizào .... soap
fēn .... Chinese money, minute
fěn .... pink
fójìao .... Buddhist
fǔbì .... Chinese money
fùjì .... remarks
fùjìn .... vicinity
fùqīn .... father
fúwùyúan .... service person

G

gāng .... steel
gāngbǐ .... pen
gānxǐ .... dry clean
gānxǐ dìan .... dry cleaner's
gāo .... tall
gàosù .... to tell
ge .... (C)
gēge .... brother
gěi .... to give
gěi qían .... to pay money
gēn .... with
gōngchǐ .... meter
gōnggòng .... public
gōnggòng dìanhùa ..... public telephone
gōnggòngqìchē .... bus

gōngjù	tool
gōnglǐ	kilometer
gōngyù	boarding room
gōngyuán	park
gǒu	dog
guāfēng	windy
gǔai wǎnr	turn the corner
guālíandāo	razor
gǔan	place, hall
gǔan	to close, closed
gǔdǒng	antique
gǔdǒng dìan	antique store
gūgu	aunt
gùi	expensive
gùitái	counter
gùizi	cupboard
gúo	nation, state
gùo	after
gúojì	international
gǔojìang	jam
gúonèi	domestic
gúowài	abroad
gùo yí kè	quarter after

H

hǎi	sea
hǎibīn	seashore
háishì	or (in questions)
hángkōngxìn	airmail
hǎo	well, good
hào	number
hē	to drink
hé	and
hēi	black
Hélán	Netherlands
hěn	very
hóng	red
hòu	thick
hòubīanr	behind
hòuchē shì	waiting room
hūa	multi-colored
hùa	language
hùai	bad
hùan (chē)	to transfer (vehicle)
húang	yellow
húangyóu	butter
hùar	picture
hūar	flower
hūar dìan	flower shop
húashì	Fahrenheit
hūayúan	garden
hūi	gray
hùi	concert, meeting, to be able to, can
húijīao	Moslem
hújīao	pepper
hǔo	fire, flame
hǔochē	train
hǔochē zhàn	train station
hùoshì	or
hǔotǔi	ham
hùzhào	passport

J

jī	chicken
jǐ	some, how many?
jì	to send (by post)
jía	home
jīajù	furniture
jīalǐ	home
jīalún	gallon
jīan	fried
jìan	to see, to meet
jīanglùo	to land
jìankǎng	healthy

jǐao	corner, Chinese money
jìao	to be called, to order
jìaotáng	church
jīa pǔ	family system
jìaqían	price
jīatíng	family
jīayóu zhàn	gas station
jīdàn	egg
jīdūjìao	Protestant
jīe	street
jīedào bàngōngshì	subdistrict office
jìn	into, in
jīn	golden
jīnglǐ	manager
jìngzi	mirror
jìnìanpǐn	souvenir
jìnìanpǐn dìan	souvenir store
jīntīan	today
jìnzhǐ tōngxíng	no trespassing
jǐu	wine, nine
jǐu gǔanr	tavern
jǐushí	ninety
jǐuyùe	September
jùyùan	theater
júzi	orange
júzishǔi	orange juice

K

kāfēi	coffee
kāfēi dìan	coffeeshop
kāfēisè	brown
kāi	to open, to boil, to depart, to leave
kāichē	to drive
kāishǐ	to start
kàn	to read
kànjìan	to see
kǎo	baked
kètīng	living room
kùai	fast
kùaichē	fast train
kùaizi	chopsticks
kùang	mineral
kùangqúanshǔi	mineral water
kùwà	pantyhose
kùzi	trousers

L

là	wax
lái	to come
láihúi	round-trip
lán	blue
lǎo	old
lèi	type
lěng	cold
lěngpán	cold dishes (appetizers)
lǐ	inside
lǐang	two
líangxíe	sandals
líanyīqún	dress
lǐfà	haircut
lǐfà dìan	hairdresser's
líng	zero
lǐngdài	tie
línyù	shower
lìshǐ	history
lìu	six
lìushí	sixty
lìuyùe	June
lóu	floor
lóudào	corridor
lù	route
lǜ	green
lǚgǔan	hotel
lǚkè	passenger, traveler, tourist

lǚxíng	travel
lǚxíng shè	travel agent
lúzi	stove

M

mai	to buy
mài	to sell
màipìan	cereal
màipìaodè	ticket-seller
mǎmǎhūhū	so-so
màn	slow
máo	Chinese money, wool
māo	cat
máojīn	towel
máoyī	sweater
màozi	hat
mǎtǒng	toilet
méi	coal
Měigúo	America
Měigúorén	American
mèimei	sister
měishùgǔan	art gallery
mén	door
ménlíng	doorbell
mǐ	rice
mì	honey
mìan	noodles
mìanbāo	bread
mìanbāo dìan	bakery
mìan gǔanr	noodle shop
mìao	temple
mǐao	seconds
míngtīan	tomorrow
míngtīan jìan	see you tomorrow
míngtīan xìawǔ jìan	see you tomorrow afternoon
míngxìnpìan	postcard
míngzi	name
mǔqīn	mother

N

nà	that, those
nǎ	which
nán	male, south
nánbīanr	South
nánfāng	southern
nánrén	man
nàozhōng	alarm clock
nǎr	where
nàr	there
náshǒucài	specialties (food)
něi	which
nèikù	underpants
nèiyī	undershirt
néng	to be able to, can
nǐ	you
nían	year
níanqīng	young
nǐao	bird
nǐde	your
Nǐ hǎo ma?	How are you?
nǐmen	you
Nín mànman chī	Good appetite
níu	cow
níunǎi	milk
níunǎi dìan	dairy
níu ròu, níuròu	beef
nǚ	female
nǔan	warm
nǚér	daughter
nǚrén	woman

O

Ōuzhōu	Europe

P

pángbīanr	next to
pánzi	plate
péngyou	friend
pí	skin, leather, peel
píanyi	inexpensive
pìao	ticket
píbāo	purse
píjiāzi	wallet
píjiu	beer
píng	bottle
píngcháng	usually
píngguǒ	apple
pō	slope
pǔtōngchē	ordinary train

Q

qī	seven
qí	astride
qīan	thousand
qían	money
qīanbǐ	pencil
qíanbīanr	in front of
qíang	wall
qíangjiao	corner
qíaokèlì	chocolate
qìchē	car
qín	musical instrument
qíng	fine, clear
qǐng	please
qǐngwèn	may I ask
qíong	poor
qìshǔi	soda pop
qíu	ball
qīutīan	autumn
qìyóu	gasoline
qiwēn	temperature
qíyùe	July
qù	to go
qúnzi	skirt

R

rè	hot
rén	person
rènhé	any
rénxíngdào	sidewalk
Rìběn	Japan
rìlì	calendar
Rìwén	Japanese
rìyòng	everyday use
róngyì	easy
ròu	meat
ròu dìan	butcher shop
rùkǒu	entrance

S

sālà	salad
sǎn	umbrella
sān	three
sānlúnchē	pedicab
sānshí	thirty
sānyùe	March
shāfā	sofa
shān	mountain
shàng	up, on, on top of, to climb, to get on
shàng (chē)	to board (vehicle)
shàngbīanr	over, above
shāngdìan	store, shop
shàngwǔ	morning
shàngyī	jacket
shǎo	few, little
shāo	roasted

sháor	spoon
shéi	who
shēng	voice
shénme	what
shénme shíhòu	when, what time
shèshì	Centigrade
shí	food, ten
shì	to be
shíbā	eighteen
shíèr	twelve
shíèryùe	December
shíhòu	time
shíjīan bǐao	time schedule
shíjiu	nineteen
shílìu	sixteen
shípǐn dìan	grocery store
shíqī	seventeen
shísān	thirteen
shísì	fourteen
shítáng	dining room
shíwǔ	fifteen
shīwùzhāolǐng	lost-and-found office
shíyīyùe	November
shíyùe	October
shōujù	receipt
shǒujùanr	handkerchief
shòupìao chù	ticket office
shòupìaoyúan	conductor
shǒutàor	gloves
shǒuyīnjī	radio
shū	book
shūazi	brush
shú cài	cooked vegetables
shū dìan	bookstore
shūfáng	study, den
shǔi	water
shùi	to sleep
shǔiguǒ	fruit
shǔiguǒ dìan	fruit store
shùipáo	bathrobe
shùiyī	pajamas
shūo	to say, to speak
shūohùa	to speak
shúshí	cold cuts
shúshí dìan	delicatessen
shūshu	uncle
shūzhūo	desk
shùzì	number
shūzi	com b
sì	four
sījī	driver
sìshí	forty
sìyùe	April
sùi	(C)
sǔo	(C)
sǔo	lock

T

tā	he, she, it, him, her
tāde	his
táidēng	lamp
tàipíng mén	emergency gate
tàiyáng	sun
tāmen	they, them
tāng	soup
tāngchí	soup spoon
tángguǒ	candy
tǎngyǐ	reclining car
táoqì	ceramics
tèbíe	special
tèkùai	express train
tīan	day
tían	sweet
tíandīan	dessert

tīanhūabǎn	ceiling
tīanqì	weather
tīantīan	everyday
tīanzhǔjìao	Catholic
tíao	(C)
tiěgǔi	track
tíng	booth
tíng chē	to park (vehicle)
tíngchē chǎng	parking lot
tínglíu	to stay
tīngtǒng	receiver
tǐwēn	body temperature
tǐyùgǔan	gymnasium
tóngzhì	comrade

W

wàigúo	foreign
wàiyī	coat
wǎn	late
wǎnfàn	dinner
wàng	to forget, toward, to
wàng chūkǒu	to the exit
wánjù	toy
wǎnshàng	evening
wǎnshàng jìan	see you in the evening
wàzi	sock
wèi	hello
wèishénme	why
wēn	warm
wén	written language
wèn	to ask
wénjù	stationery
wénjù dìan	stationery store
wèntí	question
wǒ	I, me
wǒde	my
wòfáng	bedroom
wǒmen	we
wòpù	sleeping car
wǔ	five
wǔfàn	dinner
wǔshí	fifty
wǔyùe	May
wūzi	room

X

xǐ	to wash
xī	west
xìa	next, down
xìa (chē)	to disembark
xìabīanr	under, below
xìan	line
xìang	elephant
xīangcháng	sausage
xīangjīao	banana
xīangshǔi	perfume
xǐang yào	would like
xīangzi	trunk, suitcase
xìanzài	now
xǐao	small
xǐaoháir	child
xǐao máojīn	hand towel
Xǐaoxīn!	Be careful!
xìatīan	summer
xìawù	foggy
xìawǔ	afternoon
xìaxǔe	snows
xìayǔ	rains
Xībānyá	Spain
xībīanr	West
xīe	several
xíe	shoes
xǐe	to write
xǐe chū	to write out

xièxie	....	thank you
xīfāng	....	western
xǐhuan	....	to like
xǐliǎn máojīn	....	washcloth
xīn	....	new
xìn	....	letter
xínglǐ	....	luggage
xīngqī	....	week
xīngqīèr	....	Tuesday
xīngqīliù	....	Saturday
xīngqīsān	....	Wednesday
xīngqīsì	....	Thursday
xīngqītiān	....	Sunday
xīngqīwǔ	....	Friday
xīngqīyī	....	Monday
xīnxiān	....	fresh
xiōngzhào	....	brassiere
xìpiào	....	theater ticket
xǐshǒuchí	....	washbasin
xǐyáng ... west ocean, a western country
xǐyī diàn	....	laundry
xìyuàn	....	theater
xǐzǎo	....	to bathe
xǐzǎofáng	....	bathroom
xǐzǎo máojīn	....	bath towel
xīzhuāng	....	suit
xúexí	....	to learn
xūezi	....	boots
xūyào	....	to need

Y

yā	....	duck
yágāo	....	toothpaste
yān	....	tobacco
yán	....	salt
yān diàn	....	tobacco store
yàng	....	kind, type
yǎnjìng	....	eyeglasses
yánsè	....	color
yán shuǐ	....	salt water
yào ... to cost, to want, must, to take (time)
yào diàn	....	pharmacy
yàofáng	....	pharmacy
yáshuā	....	toothbrush
yè	....	page
yè, yèlǐ	....	night
yě	....	also
yī	....	one
yí	....	one
yì	....	one
yī, yīfú	....	clothing
yǐ, yǐzi	....	chair
yìbǎi	....	one hundred
yīchú	....	clothes closet
Yìdàlì	....	Italy
yìdiǎnr	....	a little
yígòng	....	altogether
yǐhòu	....	later
yí kè	....	one quarter
Yílùpíngān!	.	Safe and peaceful journey!
yìngbì	....	coin
yìnggāi	....	to have to, should
Yīngguó	....	England
Yīngwén	....	English
yínháng	....	bank
yǐnliào	....	beverage
yínqì	....	silver
yīnyùe	....	music
yìqian	....	one thousand
yǐqián	....	before
yīshēng	....	doctor
yíyàng	....	same
yīyuàn	....	hospital

yíyùe	....	January
yìzhí zǒu	....	straight ahead
yòngpǐn	....	goods
yǒu	.... to have, there is, there are
yòu	....	right
yòubiānr	....	right, right side
yóujiàn	....	mail
yóujú	....	post office
yóupiào	....	stamp
yǒuqián	....	rich
yǒurén	....	occupied
yóutǒng	....	mailbox
yǒuyìsi	....	interesting
yóuyǒng chí	....	swimming pool
yóuyǒngyī	....	swimsuit
yóuzhèng	....	postal
yú	....	fish
yúan	..... unit of Chinese currency
yú diàn	....	fish store
yùe	....	month
yùetái	....	platform
yún	....	cloud
yúxiā lèi	....	seafood
yǔyī	....	raincoat

Z

zá	....	mixed
záhùo	....	miscellaneous goods
záhùo diàn	....	drugstore
zài	.. is (in, on, at), are (in, on, at), again
zài jiàn	....	see you again
zài shǔo	....	to repeat
zǎofàn	....	breakfast
zázhì	....	magazine
zěnme	....	how
zhá	....	fried
zhàn	....	stop, station, to stand
zhǎng	....	(C)
zhàng	....	account
zhàngdān	....	bill
zhǎnlǎnguǎn	....	exhibition hall
zhànxiàn	....	the line is busy
zhǎo	....	to look for
zhàopiàn	....	photo
zhàoxiàngjī	....	camera
zhàoxiàng qìcái diàn	.....	camera store
zhè	....	this, these
zhèi	....	this, these
zhēng	....	steamed
zhèngcháng	....	normal
zhèngquè	....	correct
zhěntóu	....	pillow
zhèr	....	here
zhǐ	....	paper, only
zhǐbì	....	paper currency
zhīdào	....	to know
zhōng	....	clock
zhōngbiǎo	....	clock, watch
zhōngbiǎo diàn	.....	watchmaker's
Zhōngguó	....	China
zhōngjiān	....	middle
zhōngtóu	....	hour
Zhōngwén	....	Chinese
zhōngyāng	....	central
zhōngyāng gōngyúan	.....	central park
zhòngyào	....	important
zhǔ	....	boiled
zhù	....	to live, to reside
zhǔan	....	to turn
zhūangyánde	....	magnificent
zhūozi	....	table
zhūròu, zhū ròu	....	pork
zìdiǎn	....	dictionary
zìdòng diàntī	....	escalator

zìxíngchē	....	bicycle
zìzhǐlǒu	....	wastebasket
zōngjiào	....	religion
zǒngzhàn	....	main station
zǒu	....	to walk
zǒu jìn	....	to enter
zǔfù	....	grandfather
zǔfùmǔ	....	grandparents
zǔmǔ	....	grandmother
zùo	....	to sit, to do, to make, by
zùo	....	(C)
zǔo	....	left
zǔobiānr	....	left, left side
zúotiān	....	yesterday
zùowèi	....	seat

GLOSSARY
English-Chinese

A

about .... chàbùduō
above .... shàngbīanr
abroad .... gúowài
account .... zhàng
after .... gùo
afternoon .... xìawǔ
again .... zài
age .... sùi
airmail .... hángkōngxìn
airplane .... fēijī
airplane ticket .... fēijīpìao
airport .... fēijīchǎng
alarm clock .... nàozhōng
a little .... yìdīar
all .... dōu
also .... yě
altogether .... yígòng
America .... Měigúo
American .... Měigúorén
and .... hé
antique .... gǔdǒng
antique store .... gǔdǒng dìan
any .... rènhé
apartment .... fáng
appetizers .... lěngpán
apple .... pínggǔo
April (in, on, at) ...... sìyuè
are (in, on, at) .... zài
arrive (inf.) .... dào
art gallery .... měishùgǔan
ask (inf.) .... wèn
aspirin .... āsīpīlín
astride .... qí
August .... báyuè
aunt .... gūgu
autumn .... qīutīan

B

bad .... bùhǎo, bù hǎo; hùai
badly .... bùhǎo, bù hǎo
baked .... kǎo
bakery .... mìanbāo dìan
ball .... qíu
banana .... xīangjīao
bank .... yínháng
basement .... dìxìashì
bathe (inf.) .... xǐzǎo
bathrobe .... shùipáo
bathroom .... xǐzǎofáng
bath towel .... xǐzǎo máojīn
be (inf.) .... shì
be able to (inf.) ...... hùi, néng
bean .... dòu
be called (inf.) .... jìao
Be careful! .... Xǐaoxīn!
bed .... chúang
bedroom .... wòfáng
beef .... níu ròu, níuròu
beer .... píjǐu
before .... chà, yǐqían
behind .... hòubīanr
Beijing .... Běijīng
below .... xìabīanr
beverage .... yǐnlìao
bicycle .... zìxíngchē
big .... dà

bill .... zhàngdān
bird .... nǐao
black .... hēi
blouse .... chènyī
blue .... lán
board (vehicle), inf. .... shàng (chē)
boarding room .... gōngyù
boat .... chúan
body temperature ...... tǐwēn
boil (inf.) .... kāi
boiled .... zhǔ
book (inf.) .... dìng
book .... shū
bookstore .... shū dìan
booth .... tíng
boots .... xūezi
bottle .... píng
boulevard .... dàdào
bound together (C) .... běn
brassiere .... xīongzhào
bread .... mìanbāo
breakfast .... zǎofàn
bring (inf.) .... dài
brother .... gēge
brown .... kāfēisè
brush .... shūazi
Buddhist .... fójìao
bus .... gōnggòngqìchē
butcher's .... ròu dìan
butter .... húangyóu
buy (inf.) .... mǎi
by .... dǎ, zùo

C

calendar .... rìlì
camera .... zhàoxiangjī
camera store ..... zhàoxìang qìcái dìan
candy .... tánggǔo
car .... chē, qìchē
carpet .... dìtǎn
cat .... māo
Catholic .... tīanzhǔjìao
ceiling .... tīanhūabǎn
Centigrade .... shèshì
central .... zhōngyāng
central park ..... zhōngyāng gōngyúan
ceramics .... táoqì
cereal .... màipìan
chair .... yǐ, yǐzi
chicken .... jī
child .... xǐaoháir
China .... Zhōnggúo
Chinese .... Zhōngwén
Chinese currency
.... fēn, fǔbì, jǐao, máo, yúan
chocolate .... qīaokèlì
chopsticks .... kùaizi
church .... jìaotáng
city .... chéngshì
clear .... qíng
climb (inf.) .... shàng
clock .... zhōng, zhōngbǐao
close (inf.) .... gǔan
closed .... gǔan
clothes closet ...... yīchú
clothing .... yī, yīfú
cloud .... yún

coal .... méi
coat .... wàiyī
coffee .... kāfēi
coffeeshop .... kāfēi dìan
coin .... yìngbì
cold .... lěng
cold cuts .... shúshí
cold dishes .... lěngpán
color .... yánsè
comb .... shūzi
come (inf.) .... lái
compartment .... chēxīang
comrade .... tóngzhì
concert .... hùi
conductor .... shòupìaoyúan
conversation .... dùihùa
cooked vegetables .... shú cài
corner .... jǐao, qíangjǐao
correct .... zhèngquè
corridor .... lóudào
cost (inf.) .... yào
counter .... gùitái
cow .... níu
cup .... bēi
cupboard .... gùizi
curtain .... chūanglían

D

dairy .... níunǎi dìan
daughter .... nǔér
day .... tīan
daytime .... báitīan
December .... shíèryuè
degree .... dù
delicatessen ..... shúshí dìan
den .... shūfáng
deodorant .... chúhànjì
depart (inf.) .... kāi
department .... bù
department store .... bǎihùo dìan
desk .... shūzhǔo
dessert .... tíandǐan
dictionary .... zìdǐan
dining room .... fàntīng, shítáng
dinner .... wǎnfàn, wǔfàn
disembark (inf.) ...... xìa (chē)
dish .... cài
do (inf.) .... zùo
doctor .... yīshēng
dog .... gǒu
domestic .... gúonèi
door .... mén
doorbell .... ménlíng
down .... xìa
dress .... líanyīqún
drink (inf.) .... hē
drive (inf.) .... kāichē
driver .... sījī
drugstore .... záhùo dìan
dry clean (inf.) ...... gānxǐ
dry cleaner's ...... gānxǐ dìan
duck .... yā

E

East .... dōngbīanr
east .... dōng
eastern .... dōngfāng

east ocean . . . . dōngyáng
easy . . . . róngyì
eat (inf.) . . . . chī
eat a meal (inf.) . . . . chīfàn
egg . . . . dàn, jīdàn
eight . . . . bā
eighteen . . . . shíbā
eighth . . . . dìbā
eighty . . . . bāshí
electrical goods . . . . dìanqì pǐn
electricity . . . . dìan
elephant . . . . xìang
emergency gate . . . . tàipíng mén
England . . . . Yīngguó
English . . . . Yīngwén
enter (inf.) . . . . zǒu jìn
entrance . . . . rùkǒu
escalator . . . . zìdòng dìantī
Europe . . . . Ōuzhōu
evening . . . . wǎnshàng
everyday . . . . tīantīan
everyday use . . . . rìyòng
excuse me . . . . duìbùqǐ
exhibition hall . . . . zhǎnlǎnguǎn
exit . . . . chūkǒu
expensive . . . . gùi
eyeglasses . . . . yǎnjìng

F

Fahrenheit . . . . húashì
family . . . . jīatíng
family system . . . . jīa pǔ
fast . . . . kùai
father . . . . fùqīn
February . . . . èryùe
female . . . . nǚ
few . . . . shǎo
fifteen . . . . shíwǔ
fifty . . . . wǔshí
film . . . . dīpìan
fine . . . . qíng
fire . . . . hǔo
fish . . . . yú
fish store . . . . yú dìan
five . . . . wǔ
flame . . . . hǔo
floor . . . . lóu
flower . . . . hǔar
flower shop . . . . hǔar dìan
fly (inf.) . . . . fēi
foggy . . . . xìawù
food . . . . shí
foreign . . . . wàigúo
forget (inf.) . . . . wàng
fork . . . . chāzi
form . . . . bīao, bīaogé
forty . . . . sìshí
four . . . . sì
fourteen . . . . shísì
France . . . . Fǎgúo
freezing point . . . . bīng dǐan
French . . . . Fǎwén
fresh . . . . xīnxīan
Friday . . . . xīngqīwǔ
fried . . . . jīan, zhá
friend . . . . péngyou
from . . . . cóng
fruit . . . . shǔiguǒ
fruit store . . . . shǔiguǒ dìan
furniture . . . . jīajù

G

gallon . . . . jīalún

garage . . . . chēfáng
garden . . . . hūayúan
gasoline . . . . qìyóu
gas station . . . . jīayóu zhàn
German . . . . Déwén
Germany . . . . Dégúo
get on (inf.) . . . . shàng
give (inf.) . . . . gěi
glass . . . . bōli, bēi, bōlibēi
gloves . . . . shǒutàor
go (inf.) . . . . qù
golden . . . . jīn
good . . . . hǎo
Good appetite! . . . . Nín mànman chī!
goods . . . . yòngpǐn
grandfather . . . . zǔfù
grandmother . . . . zǔmǔ
grandparents . . . . zǔfùmǔ
grass . . . . cǎo
gray . . . . hūi
green . . . . lǜ
grocery store . . . . shípǐn dìan
gymnasium . . . . tǐyùguǎn

H

haircut . . . . lǐfà
hairdresser's . . . . lǐfà dìan
half . . . . bàn
hall . . . . guǎn
ham . . . . hǔotǔi
handkerchief . . . . shǒujùanr
hand towel . . . . xīao máojīn
hat . . . . màozi
have (inf.) . . . . yǒu
have to (inf.) . . . . yīnggāi
he . . . . tā
healthy . . . . jìankāng
hello . . . . wèi
her . . . . tā
here . . . . zhèr
him . . . . tā
his . . . . tāde
history . . . . lìshǐ
home . . . . jīa, jīalǐ
honey . . . . mì
hospital . . . . yīyùan
hot . . . . rè
hotel . . . . lǚguǎn
hour . . . . zhōngtóu
house . . . . fángzi
how . . . . zěnme
How are you? . . . . Nǐ hǎo ma?
how many . . . . jǐ
how much . . . . dūoshǎo
hundred . . . . bǎi
　　one hundred . . . . yìbǎi
hungry . . . . è

I

I . . . . wǒ
ice . . . . bīng
important . . . . zhòngyào
in . . . . jìn
inexpensive . . . . píanyi
in front of . . . . qíanbīanr
inside . . . . lǐ
interesting . . . . yǒuyìsi
international . . . . gúojì
into . . . . jìn
is (in, on, at) . . . . zài
it . . . . tā
Italy . . . . Yìdàlì

J

jacket . . . . shàngyī
jam . . . . gǔojìang
January . . . . yíyùe
Japan . . . . Rìběn, dōngyáng
Japanese . . . . Rìwén
July . . . . qíyùe
June . . . . lìuyùe

K

kilometer . . . . gōnglǐ
kind . . . . yàng
kitchen . . . . chúfáng
knife . . . . dāozi
know (inf.) . . . . zhīdào

L

lacking . . . . chà
lamp . . . . táidēng
land (inf.) . . . . jìanglùo
language . . . . hùa
late . . . . wǎn
later . . . . yǐhòu
laundry . . . . xǐyī dìan
lavatory . . . . cèsǔo
learn (inf.) . . . . xúexí
leather . . . . pí
leave (inf.) . . . . kāi
left . . . . zǔo, zǔobīanr
left side . . . . zǔobīanr
letter . . . . xìn
light . . . . dēng
like (inf.) . . . . xǐhuan
line . . . . xìan
little . . . . shǎo
live (inf.) . . . . zhù
living room . . . . kètīng
lock . . . . sǔo
long . . . . cháng
look for (inf.) . . . . zhǎo
lose (inf.) . . . . dīu
lost-and-found office . . . shīwùzhǎolǐng
low . . . . dī
luggage . . . . xínglǐ

M

magazine . . . . zázhì
magnificent . . . . zhǔangyánde
mail . . . . yóujìan
mailbox . . . . yóutǒng
mainland . . . . dàlù
main station . . . . zǒngzhàn
make (inf.) . . . . zùo
make (telephone call), inf. . . . . dǎ
male . . . . nán
man . . . . nánrén
manager . . . . jīnglǐ
many . . . . dūo
map . . . . dìtú
March . . . . sānyùe
market . . . . càichǎng
May . . . . wǔyùe
me . . . . wǒ
meal . . . . fàn
meat . . . . ròu
meet (inf.) . . . . jìan
meeting . . . . hùi
menu . . . . càidān
meter . . . . gōngchǐ
middle . . . . zhōngjīan
milk . . . . níunǎi
mineral . . . . kùang

mineral water .... kuàngquánshǔi
minute .... fēn
mirror .... jìngzi
miscellaneous goods .... záhùo
mixed .... zá
Monday .... xīngqīyī
money .... qián
money-exchange office .... dùihùan chù
month .... yùe
morning .... shàngwǔ
Moslem .... húijìao
mother .... mǔqīn
mountain .... shān
movie .... dìanyǐng
movie theater .... dìanyǐngyùan
much .... dūo
multi-colored .... hūa
museum .... bówùgǔan
music .... yīnyùe
musical instrument .... qín
must .... yào
my .... wǒde

N

name .... míngzi
napkin .... cānjīn
nation .... gúo
need (inf.) .... xūyào
Netherlands .... Hélán
new .... xīn
newspaper .... bàozhǐ
next .... xìa
next to .... pángbīanr
night .... yè, yèlǐ
nine .... jǐu
nineteen .... shíjǐu
ninety .... jǐushí
noodles .... mìan
noodle shop .... mìan gǔanr
normal .... zhèngcháng
North .... běibīanr
north .... běi
northern .... běifāng
not .... bù, bú
not good .... bùhǎo, bù hǎo
no trespassing .... jìnzhǐ tōngxíng
November .... shíyīyùe
now .... xìanzài
number .... hào, shùzì

O

o'clock .... dǐan
occupied .... yǒurén
October .... shíyùe
office .... bàngōngshì
often .... cháng, chángcháng
old .... lǎo
on .... shàng
one .... yī, yí, yì
one-way .... dānchéng
only .... zhǐ
on top of .... shàng
open (inf.) .... kāi, dǎkāi
or .... hùoshì
or (in questions) .... háishì
orange .... júzi
orange juice .... júzishǔi
order (inf.) .... jìao
ordinary train .... pǔtōngchē
oriental .... dōngfāng
oriental goods .... dōngfāng hùo
out .... chū
over .... shàngbīanr

P

page .... yè
pajamas .... shùiyī
pantyhose .... kùwà
paper .... zhǐ
paper currency .... zhǐbì
parcel .... bāogǔo
park (vehicle), inf. .... tíng chē
park .... gōngyúan
parking lot .... tíngchē chǎng
passenger .... lǚkè
passport .... hùzhào
pastry .... dǐanxīn
pay money (inf.) .... gěi qián
pedicab .... sānlúnchē
peel .... pí
pen .... gāngbǐ
pencil .... qīanbǐ
people .... rén
pepper .... hújīao
perfume .... xīangshǔi
person .... rén
pharmacy .... yào dìan, yàofáng
photo .... zhàopìan
picture .... hùar
pillow .... zhěntou
pink .... fěn
place .... dìfāng, gǔan
plate .... pánzi
platform .... yùetái
please .... qǐng
pool .... chí
poor .... qíong
porcelain .... cíqì
pork .... zhūròu, zhū ròu
postal .... yóuzhèng
postcard .... míngxìnpìan
post office .... yóujú
pound .... bàng
price .... jìaqían
Protestant .... jīdūjìao
public .... gōnggòng
purse .... píbāo

Q

quarter .... yí kè
quarter after .... gùo yí kè
quarter to .... chà yí kè
question .... wèntí
quilt .... bèi

R

radio .... shōuyīnjī
raincoat .... yǔyī
rains .... xìayǔ
razor .... gūalǐandāo
read (inf.) .... kàn
receipt .... shōujù
receiver .... tīngtǒng
record .... chàngpìan
red .... hóng
refrigerator .... bīngxīang
religion .... zōngjìao
remarks .... fùjì
repeat (inf.) .... zài shūo
reserve (inf.) .... dìng
reside (inf.) .... zhù
restaurant .... fàngǔanr
rice .... fàn, mǐ
rich .... yǒuqían
right .... yòu, yòubīanr
right side .... yòubīanr

S

roasted .... shāo
room ...... fáng, fángjīan, wūzi
round-trip .... láihúi
route .... lù

S

Safe and peaceful journey! .. Yílùpíngān!
salad .... sālà
salt .... yán
salt water .... yán shǔi
same .... yíyàng
sandals .... líangxíe
Saturday .... xīngqīlìu
sausage .... xīangcháng
say (inf.) .... shūo
schedule .... bǐao, bǐaogé
sea .... hǎi
seafood .... yúxīa lèi
seashore .... hǎibīn
seat .... zùowèi
second-class .... èr děng
seconds .... mǐao
see (inf.) ...... jìan, kànjìan
  see you again .... zài jìan
  see you in the evening . wǎnshàng jìan
  see you tomorrow ... míngtīan jìan
  see you tomorrow afternoon
  .... míngtīan xìawǔ jìan
sell (inf.) .... mài
send (by post), inf. .... jì
September .... jǐuyùe
service person .... fúwùyúan
seven .... qī
seventeen .... shíqī
seventh .... dìqī
several .... xīe
she .... tā
shirt .... chènyī
shoes .... xíe
shop .... dìan
short .... ǎi, dǔan
shower .... línyù
sick .... bìng
side .... bīanr
sidewalk .... rénxíngdào
silver .... yínqì
sister .... mèimei
sit (inf.) .... zùo
six .... lìu
sixteen .... shílìu
sixty .... lìushí
size .... dàxǐao
skin .... pí
skirt .... qúnzi
sleep (inf.) .... shùi
slip .... chènqún
slip of paper .... dǎnzi
slope .... pō
slow .... màn
small .... xǐao
smoke (inf.) .... chōuyān
snows .... xìaxǔe
soap .... féizào
socks .... wàzi
soda pop .... qìshǔi
sofa .... shāfā
some .... jǐ
son .... érzi
so-so .... mǎmǎhūhū
soup .... tāng
soup spoon .... tāngchí
South .... nánbīanr
south .... nán

111

southern	....	nánfāng
souvenir	....	jìnìanpǐn
souvenir store	....	jìnìanpǐn dìan
Spain	....	Xībānyá
speak (inf.)	....	shūo, shūohùa
special	....	tèbíe
specialties (food)	....	náshǒucài
spoon	....	sháor
spring	....	chūntīan
stamp	....	yóupìao
stand (inf.)	....	zhàn
start (inf.)	....	kāishǐ
state	....	gúo
station	....	zhàn
stationery	....	wénjù
stationery store	....	wénjù dìan
stay (inf.)	....	tínglíu
steamed	....	zhēng
steel	....	gāng
stir-fried	....	chǎo
stop (vehicle)	....	chē zhàn
stop	....	zhàn
store	....	dìan, shāngdìan
stove	....	lúzi
straight ahead	....	yìzhí zǒu
street	....	jīe
study	....	shūfáng
subdistrict office	....	jīedào bàngōngshì
subway	....	dìxìatǐedàochē
suit	....	xīzhūang
suitcase	....	xīangzi
summer	....	xìatīan
sun	....	tàiyáng
Sunday	....	xīngqǐtīan
sweater	....	máoyī
sweet	....	tían
swimming pool	....	yóuyǒng chí
swimsuit	....	yóuyǒngyī

T

table	....	zhūozi
tailor's	....	cáiféng dìan
take (time), inf.	....	yào
tall	....	gāo
tavern	....	jǐu gǔanr
taxi	....	chūzuchē
tea	....	chá
teacup	....	chábēi
teahouse	....	chágǔan
telegram	....	dìanbào
telephone	....	dìanhùa
public telephone	...	gōnggòng dìanhùa
telephone book	....	dìanhùa bù
telephone booth	....	dìanhùa tíng
telephone call	....	dìanhùa
local telephone call	....	běndì dìanhùa
long-distance telephone call		
	....	chángtú dìanhùa
television	....	dìanshì
tell (inf.)	....	gàosù
temperature	....	qìwēn
temple	....	mìao
ten	....	shí
thank you	....	xìexie
that	....	nà
theater	....	jùyùan, xìyùan
theater ticket	....	xìpìao
them	....	tāmen
there	....	nàr
there is, there are	....	yǒu
these	....	zhè, zhèi
they	....	tāmen
thick	....	hòu

thin	....	báo
thing	....	dōngxi, bǎihùo
thirteen	....	shísān
thirty	....	sānshí
this	....	zhè, zhèi
those	....	nà
thousand	....	qīan
one thousand	....	yìqīan
three	....	sān
Thursday	....	xīngqīsì
ticket	....	pìao
ticket office	....	shòupìao chù
ticket-seller	....	màipìaodè
tie	....	lǐngdài
time	....	shíhòu
time schedule	....	shíjīan bǐao
to	....	dào, wàng
tobacco	....	yān
tobacco store	....	yān dìan
today	....	jīntīan
toilet	....	mǎtǒng
tomorrow	....	míngtīan
tool	....	gōngjù
toothbrush	....	yáshūa
toothpaste	....	yágāo
tourist	....	lǚkè
toward	....	wàng
towel	....	máojīn
toy	....	wánjù
track	....	tǐegǔi
train	....	hǔochē
dining car	....	cānchē
express train	....	tèkùai
fast train	....	kùaichē
reclining car	....	tǎngyī
sleeping car	....	wòpù
train station	....	hǔochē zhàn
transfer (vehicle), inf.	....	hùan (chē)
travel (inf.)	....	dǎ
travel	....	lǚxíng
travel agent	....	lǚxíng shè
traveler	....	lǚkè
trolley	....	dìanchē
trousers	....	kùzi
trunk	....	xīangzi
Tuesday	....	xīngqīèr
turn (inf.)	....	zhǔan
turn the corner	....	gǔai wǎnr
twelve	....	shíèr
twenty	....	èrshí
two	....	èr, lǐang
type	....	lèi, yàng
typical	....	dǐanxíng

U

umbrella	....	sǎn
uncle	....	shūshu
under	....	xìabīanr
underpants	....	nèikù
undershirt	....	nèiyī
understand (inf.)	....	dǒng
up	....	shàng
usually	....	píngcháng

V

vegetable	....	cài
vegetable store	....	cài dìan
vehicle	....	chē
verb	....	dòngcí
very	....	hěn
vicinity	....	fùjìn
voice	....	shēng

W

waiting room	....	hòuchē shì
walk (inf.)	....	zǒu
wall	....	qíang
wallet	....	píjīazi
want (inf.)	....	yào
warm	....	nǔan, wēn
wash (inf.)	....	xǐ
washbasin	....	xǐshǒuchí
washcloth	....	xǐlian máojīn
wastebasket	....	zìzhǐlǒu
watch	....	bǐao, zhōngbǐao
watchmaker's	....	zhōngbǐao dìan
water	....	shǔi
wax	....	là
ways	....	fāngfǎ
we	....	wǒmen
weather	....	tīanqì
Wednesday	....	xīngqǐsān
week	....	xīngqī
well	....	hǎo
West	....	xībīanr
west	....	xī
western	....	xīfāng
western country	....	xīyáng
west ocean	....	xīyáng
what	....	shénme
when	....	shénme shíhòu
where	....	nǎr
which	....	nǎ, něi
white	....	bái
who	....	shéi
why	....	wèishénme
window	....	chūanghù
windy	....	gǔafēng
wine	....	jǐu
winter	....	dōngtīan
with	....	gēn
woman	....	nǔrén
wool	....	máo
word	....	cí
write (inf.)	....	xīe
write out (inf.)	....	xīe chū
writing instrument	....	bǐ
written language	....	wén

Y

year	....	nían
yellow	....	húang
yesterday	....	zúotīan
you	....	nǐ, nǐmen
young	....	níanqīng
your	....	nǐde

Z

zero	....	líng
zoo	....	dòngwùyúan

Càidān
menu

FANGUAR

Zùo fǎ (ways of preparation)

mìan tūo	in batter
zhǔ	boiled
kǎo	baked
shāo	roasted
zhēng	steamed
pēng	braised
zhà	fried, deep-fried
chǎo	stir-fried

Chángyòngde (general)

yán	salt
hújiao	pepper
yóu	oil
cù	vinegar
jiemò	mustard
jiangyóu	soy sauce
táng	sugar

| cài bāo | steamed bun with vegetables |
| zhīmá bǐng | sesame crisp cake |

Yǐnliao (beverages)

chá	tea
kāfēi	coffee
níunǎi	milk
jǐu	wine
pǐjǐu	beer
júzishǔi	orange juice
kùangqúanshǔi	mineral water

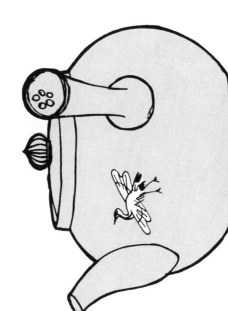

Nín mànman chī!

Qīngcài lèi (vegetables)

dòuyá	bean sprouts
sǔn	bamboo shoots
cōng	green onions
jiāng	ginger
qíncài	celery
báicài	cabbage
bōcài	spinach
shēngcài	lettuce
mógū	mushrooms
húanggūa	cucumbers
bīandòu	beans
wāndòu	peas

Shǔigǔo (fruit)

júzi	orange
lǐzi	plum
táozi	peach
xiāngjiao	banana
míjú	tangerine
bíqi	water chestnuts
mánggǔo	mango
wúhúagǔo	figs
lìzhī	litchee
yīngtáo	cherries
píngǔo	apple
meízi	prune
pútao	grapes
zǎozi	dates
níngméng	lemon
yángmeí	strawberries
mùmei	raspberries

Dīanxīn lèi (pastries)

| dòushā bāo | steamed bun with red-bean paste |

Mǐan fàn lèi (rice and noodles)

- **bái fàn** — plain rice
- **dàn chǎo fàn** — fried rice with egg
- **jī sī mian** — noodles with shredded chicken
- **ròu sī mian** — noodles with shredded pork
- **xiārén mian** — noodles with shrimp
- **dōnggū mian** — noodles with mushrooms
- **zhū gān mian** — noodles with pork liver
- **sùcài mian** — noodles with vegetables
- **chǎo mian** — fried noodles
- **xiārén chǎo mian** — fried noodles with shrimp

Lěngpán lèi (cold dishes)

- **báiqiējī** — cold chicken
- **wǔxiāng yā** — spicy duck
- **yóu bào xiā** — oil-fried shrimp
- **xūn yú** — smoked fish
- **wǔxiāng niúròu** — spiced beef
- **xián dàn** — preserved egg
- **yánshuǐ yā** — salted duck
- **bàn hǎizhé** — fish jelly
- **là cài** — hot, pickled mustard greens
- **xián huāshēng** — salted peanuts

Tāng lèi (soup)

- **qīngcài dòufu tāng** — bean curd and vegetable soup
- **báicài tāng** — cabbage soup
- **xīhóngshì dàn tāng** — tomato and egg soup
- **dōngguā tāng** — winter melon soup
- **niúròu tāng** — beef soup
- **xièròu tāng** — crab soup
- **jī tāng** — chicken soup
- **bèiké tāng** — scallop soup
- **zhàcài tāng** — vegetable soup
- **dàn huā tāng** — egg flower soup
- **yú tāng** — fish soup

Zhūròu lèi (pork)

- **tāng cù páigǔ** — sweet-and-sour spareribs
- **tāng cù lǐjī** — sweet-and-sour pork
- **shīzitóu** — pork meatballs
- **qīngjiāo ròu sī** — shredded pork with green pepper
- **gānzhá zhūpái** — fried pork fillet
- **chǎo zhū gān** — stir-fried pork liver
- **chǎo yāohuar** — stir-fried pork kidney

Niúròu lèi (beef)

- **tāng cù niúròu wán** — sweet-and-sour meatballs
- **chǎo niúròu sī** — stir-fried beef shreds
- **gānbiàn niúròu sī** — dry stir-fried beef shreds
- **niúròu yángcōng** — fried beef with onions
- **hóngshāo niúròu** — beef stew in soy sauce
- **niúròu gài láncài** — fried beef with broccoli
- **gālí niúròu** — curried beef

Jīyā lèi (poultry)

- **jī** — chicken
- **yā** — duck
- **ānchún** — quail
- **yěji** — pheasant
- **huǒji** — turkey
- **é** — goose
- **gēzi** — pigeon
- **chǎo jī sī** — fried chicken shreds
- **jī sī chǎo sǔn** — fried chicken shreds with bamboo shoots
- **gālí jī** — curried chicken
- **kǎo yā** — glazed duck

Yúxiā lèi (seafood)

- **tǎyú** — sole
- **guìyú** — salmon
- **guìyú** — Mandarin fish
- **jìyú** — perch
- **xǔeyú** — cod
- **lǐyú** — carp
- **píngyú** — turbot
- **pángxiè** — crab
- **háo** — oysters
- **shànbèiké** — scallops
- **xiā** — shrimp
- **lóngxiā** — lobster
- **dàxiā** — prawns
- **zhá dàxiā** — fried prawns
- **chǎo xiā piàn** — stir-fried sliced prawns
- **peng dàxiā** — braised prawns
- **zhá yú tiáor** — fried fish slices
- **tāng cù yú** — sweet-and-sour fish
- **hóngshāo yú** — sautéed fish in soy sauce
- **qīngzheng yú** — steamed fish
- **tāng cù lǐyú** — sweet-and-sour carp
- **tāng cù huáng yú** — sweet-and-sour yellow fish
- **qīngzheng xiè** — steamed crab
- **xiè fěn cáixīn** — crab with vegetables
- **miàn tuo xiè** — fried crab in batter
- **fúróng xiè** — crab with egg
- **zhāngchá yā** — fried duck in spices
- **cùipí yā** — crispy duck

Dòufu lèi (bean curd)

- **hóngshāo dòufu** — bean curd with soy sauce
- **mápó dòufu** — bean curd with pepper
- **dōnggū dòufu** — bean curd with mushrooms
- **xiārén dòufu** — bean curd with shrimp

(jee-ow) **jìao**	*(li)* **lái**
(my) **mǎi**	*(chee-yew)* **qù**
(shwo) **shūo**	*(yoh)* **yǒu**
(joo) **zhù**	*(ssee-yew-eh-ssee)* **xúexí**
(jee-ow) **jìao**	*(ssee-ahng)* *(yow)* **xǐang yào**
(teeng-lee-oh) **tínglíu**	*(ssee-yew-yow)* **xūyào**

to come	to be called
to go	to buy
to have	to speak
to learn	to live/reside
would like	to order
to need	to stay

(my) **mài**	*(shwo)* **shūo**
(kahn-jee-ahn) **kànjìan**	*(chr)* **chī**
(jee) **jì**	*(huh)* **hē**
(shway) **shùi**	*(jahn)* **zhàn**
(jow) **zhǎo**	*(dwong)* **dǒng**
(dah) **dǎ**	*(zi)* *(shwo)* **zài shūo**

to say	to sell
to eat	to see
to drink	to send
to stand	to sleep
to understand	to look for
to repeat	to make (telephone call, telegram)

(kahn) **kàn**	*(ssee-eh)* **xǐe**
(shr) **shì**	*(gay)* **gěi**
(yow) **yào**	*(gay)* *(chee-ahn)* **gěi qían**
(fay) **fēi**	*(nung)* **néng**
(zwo) **zùo**	*(yeeng-gi)* **yīnggāi**
(ki-chuh) **kāichē**	*(jr-dow)* **zhīdào**

to write	to read
to give	to be
to pay	to take (time)
to be able to/can	to fly
to have to/should	to sit
to know	to drive

(zoh) **zǒu**	*(ki-shr)* **kāishǐ**
(zoh) *(jeen)* **zǒu jìn**	*(ki)* **kāi**
(ssee-ah) *(chuh)* **xìa (chē)**	*(zwo-fahn)* **zùofàn**
(shahng) *(chuh)* **shàng (chē)**	*(jee-ahng-lwo)* **jìanglùo**
(hwahn) *(chuh)* **hùan (chē)**	*(deeng)* **dìng**
(dow) **dào**	*(yow)* *(chee-ahn)* **yào _____ qían** (?)

to start	to walk
to open	to enter
to cook	to disembark
to land	to board
to reserve	to transfer
to cost	to arrive

(gwahn) **gūan**	*(ki)* **kāi**
(ssee) **xǐ**	*(lew-sseeng)* **lǚxíng**
(hwahn-chee-ahn) **hùanqían**	*(choh-yahn)* **chōuyān**
(dee-oh) **dīu**	*(wuhn)* **wèn**
(wo) *(shr)* **wǒ shì**	*(ssee-ah-ssee-yew-eh)* *(luh)* **Xìaxǔe le.**
(wo-muhn) *(shr)* **wǒmen shì**	*(ssee-ah-yew)* *(luh)* **Xìayǔ le.**

to depart	to close
to travel	to wash
to smoke	to exchange money
to ask	to lose
It is snowing.	I am
It is raining.	we are

(gow) *(dee)* **gāo - dī**	*(tah)* *(shr)* **tā shì**
(chee-wong) *(yoh-chee-ahn)* **qíong - yǒuqían**	*(nee-muhn)* *(shr)* **nǐmen shì**
(dwahn) *(chahng)* **dǔan - cháng**	*(tah-muhn)* *(shr)* **tāmén shì**
(beeng) *(jee-ahn-keeng)* **bìng - jìankāng**	*(zi)* *(jee-ahn)* **Zài jìan.**
(pee-ahn-yee) *(gway)* **píanyi - gùi**	*(yoh)* **yǒu**
(low) *(nee-ahn-cheeng)* **lǎo - níanqīng**	*(nee)* *(how)* *(mah)* **Nǐ hǎo ma?**

he
she $\Big\}$ is
it

high - low

you are

poor - rich

they are

short - long

See you again.

sick - healthy

there is/there are

cheap - expensive

How are you?

old - young

(kwy) *(mahn)* **kùai - màn**	*(how)* *(hwy)* **hǎo - hùai**
(hoh) *(bow)* **hòu - báo**	*(roo-ahn)* *(yeeng)* **rǔan - yìng**
(dwo) *(show)* **dūo - shǎo**	*(gow)* *(i)* **gāo - ǎi**
(roo-koh) *(choo-koh)* **rùkǒu - chūkǒu**	*(ruh)* *(lung)* **rè - lěng**
(tee-ahn) *(swahn)* **tían - sūan**	*(zwo)* *(yoh)* **zǔo - yòu**
(dway-boo-chee) **dùibùqǐ**	*(shahng)* *(ssee-ah)* **shàng - xìa**

good - bad	fast - slow
soft - hard	thick - thin
tall - short	a lot - a little
hot - cold	entrance - exit
left - right	sweet - sour
above - below	excuse me